A Beginner's *Guide*

Published in 2022 by Birdfish Books
www.birdfishbooks.com

All rights reserved. No part of this edition
of this text may be reproduced or transmitted
in any form or by any means, electronic
or mechanical, including photocopy, recording
or any informational storage and retrieval system,
without prior permission from the publisher.

Cover image: *Yeoman's Bay* (detail), by Joshua Yeldham

ISBN-13: 978-0-6453923-0-2

BIRDFISH BOOKS

A Beginner's Guide

Poems

MARK TREDINNICK

2022

In memory of Don O'Brien
and Barry Lopez

For my parents,
Heather and Bruce Tredinnick,
and for Jodie Williams

Acknowledgements

SOME THANKS. For friendship and guidance and conversations in poetry, Steve Armstrong. These poems go back many years, and so do other friendships that have sustained me and these poems: Roland Hemmert, Chloe Watfern, Steve Meyrick, Noelia Ramon, Fernanda Penaloza, Jo Gardiner, Don O'Brien, Julie Perrin, John Foulcher, Linsay and John Knight, Brigitte Ross, Mel Greblo, Donna Ward, Ali Whitelock, Major and Didi Jackson, Judith Nangala Crispin, Denise O'Hagan, Debbie Lim, Kevin Smith, Peter Zawal, Ed Annand and Holly High, Peter Ramm, Peter Bishop, Alan Holley, Tegan Gigante, Brian Walters, Colin Milner, Barry Lopez, Cheryl O'Byrne, Calvin Bowman, Gerhard Bachfischer. Thanks, too, to my students, my mentees, and my readers. Thanks to Jidi Majia and Hunter and Hu Jia and everyone at the Lu Xun Academy in China, and to Stella and others at the Miluo International Poetry Festival.

Poetry sustains humanity, but it does not always soothe those who make it, nor make them easy to be with. I thank those who have borne me love; I wish I could have earned it better. I thank my children, in particular: Michael, Louisa, Henry, Daniel, and Lucy.

I thank my partner, Jodie Williams: *after years, at last, my heart's at peace with you.* All the years I speak of here were not years I spent with you, but I found my way in the end: *eyes like the tundra, a smile like the steppe.*

I'm grateful to Tegan Gigante at Birdfish, for taking on this book and making it so fine an object. Thank you for treating my work with such respect and helping me understand it better; thanks, too, for your patient marathon of design and typesetting.

For his permission to use detail from the painting "Yeoman's Bay" for my cover, I thank Joshua and Jo Yeldham. There are aspects of Josh's work—the engagement with place, the intricacy and largeness of scale, the intimacy and ultimacy—which I love very deeply, and which I attempt in my own life and work. There is a confluence of innocence and experience, of levity and gravity, of young and old, of anima and animus, in Josh's work that I'm engaged with in this collection.

Some of these poems have appeared—sometimes in different forms and under other titles—in journals and books and newspapers; some have appeared online. Some of them won or shortlisted in prizes. Some were commissioned. My gratitude to the editors and sponsors, publishers, festivals, and judges for their support for poetry, and for my work, and for their permission to reprint the poems here. It's possible I have forgotten where some of these poems appeared. Do forgive me any such oversights.

"Before the Day": won the inaugural Miluo River International Poetry Prize, January 2021.
"Jazz": *EXT2012, Writing Inspired by Music*, Miriam Zolin (Ed.), Extempore, 2012.
"The Lyrebird": *The Lyrebird & Other Poems*, Picaro Poets, Ginninderra, 2017; 2022; first published as Wagtail 106, 2011.
"Whitefaced Heron on the Bong Bong Flats": *The Sydney Morning Herald*, 6–8 April 2012.
"The Artist & His Model": *Australian Poetry Journal*, Vol. 2, No. 2, 2012.
"The News (Poetry Tells)": *Eureka Street*, 18 September 2012.
"You Over There, Me Here": Longlisted in the Montreal International Poetry Prize, 2011.
"Skipping the Rope": *Almost Everything I Know*, Flying Island, 2015.
"The Sword & The Pen": *The Lyrebird & Other Poems*, Ginninderra, 2011; 2017; 2022.
"Splitting Wood": *Prayers of a Secular World*, Jordie Albiston and Kevin Brophy, Inkermann & Blunt, 2016.
"The Reader": shortlisted for the ACU Poetry Prize in 2013.
"No Words": shortlisted for the ACU Poetry Prize 2021.
"The Child & Time": won the Gwen Harwood Poetry Prize in 2005; *Island*, Issue 106, September 2006.
"You Know How This Goes": *Snorkel*, No. 11, April 2010.
"Amen: A Moment of the World": *An Alphabet of Men*, Miriam Hechtman and Daragh Byrne (Eds.), Ginninderra, forthcoming.
"Ubirr": was shortlisted for the ABR (now the Peter Porter) Poetry Prize in 2005; *Australian Book Review*, No. 265, March 2005.
"Four Reservoir Tanka": *The Blue Nib*, December 2020.
"We Are Not Finished at the Skin": *PAN (Philosophy, Activism, Nature)*, Issue 4, 2007.
"Five Soft Nets": commissioned by the South Coast Writers Centre (SCWC) for use in a mural

on the wall of their new office in Coledale; *Legacies*, Sarah Nicholson and Lore White (Eds.), 2021.

"The Godwit Shores": *Live Encounters*, May 2021.

"Flood Tide": published as "Late Light with Whitefaced Herons" in *StylusLit* No. 8, September 2020.

"Ghazal of the Weather Upon the Lake": longlisted for the ACU Poetry Prize, 2021; *Resilience*, ACU, Sydney, 2021.

"Flat Rock, September": the Blake Poetry Prize 2021; published online at westwords.com.

"Inland": *Manoa* 18, No. 2, 2006; *Here: Poems for the Planet*, Elizabeth Coleman (Ed.), Copper Canyon, 2018.

"Up": longlisted in the University of Canberra Vice Chancellor's International Poetry Prize, 2015; *Underneath*, Owen Bullock and Niloofar Fanaiyan (Eds.), Axon, 2015.

"The Halflife of Coal": A Slow Combusting Hymn Kit Kelen and Jean Kent (Eds.), Flying Island, Newcastle, 2015.

"Revelation Days": *Red Room Poetry*, December 2020.

"The Jetty": Indigo, Summer, No. 6, 2011; *The Lyrebird & Other Poems*, Ginninderra, Adelaide, 2011; 2017; 2022.

"The Bay": longlisted for the Montreal International Poetry Prize, 2011.

"Tropicbird": *Almost Everything I Know*, Flying Island, 2015.

"Late Spring Snow, Reno": shortlisted for the ACU Poetry Prize, 2014; *The Language of Compassion*, ACU, Sydney, 2014.

"Rain at Eltham": shortlisted for the Rosemary Dobson Poetry Award, 2010.

"Mecca": *Wet Ink*, No. 7, December 2009. *The Lyrebird*, Wagtail 106, Picaro Press, 2011.

"With Sarasvati Under the Lemon-Scented Gum Tonight": *Poetry London*, No. 72, Summer 2012.

"Peregrine Moon": *The Australian*, 4 July 2015.

"The Last Day": *Terrain*, No. 27, Spring/Summer 2011.

"In Medias Res": longlisted in the ACU Poetry Prize 2021; *Resilience*, ACU, Sydney, 2021.

"Catullus, at Dusk, Lustful and Heartbroken, Tries His Hand at Haiku": *Egret in a Ploughed Field*, Chinese University Press, Hong Kong, 2017.

"Shreds": shortlisted in the ACU Poetry Prize 2016; *Loving Kindness*, ACU, Melbourne, 2016.

"The Propinquity of Snow": shortlisted for the Ron Pretty Poetry Prize 2015.

"Landscape with Laptop": *Contrapasso*, Issue 3, 2013.
"I Ran So Far": *Australian Poetry Journal*, Vol. 1, No. 1, 2011.
"Fog Lies": *Five Bells*, Vol. 17, No. 4, Spring 2010; *The Lyrebird*, Wagtail 106, Picaro Press, 2011.
"At Home on a Sunday Trying to Find Nothing to Do": shortlisted in the Blake Poetry Prize, 2011.
"Transit of Venus": *Eureka Street*, Vol. 22, No.18, September 2022; *Best Australian Poems 2012*.
"Black Swan Moment": *StylusLit*, No. 8, September 2020.
"Nine Pines on Kangaloon": *Flourishing Terrains: Poems for Debbie*, Stuart Cooke (Ed.), 2018.
"The Nature of All Things": *Anthology: Gardening the Future. An Essay in Plants, Poetry and Image*, TCL, Melbourne, 2016.
"The Gardens of Beijing": *So Far: Poems for Jodie*, Birdfish Books, Castlemaine, 2019.
"The Love Song of the Forest & The Field": *Poem & Dish*, 26 September 2014.
"Why You're Here: In Case One Day You Need to Know": *The Blue Nib*, December 2020.
"Page One": *So Far: Poems for Jodie*, Birdfish Books, Castlemaine, 2019.

Contents

Foreword

A Beginner's Guide	19

Prologue

Standing	31

One—Last *Things* First

An Old Lament	35
Several Birds and a Dog	36
Before the Day	37
What Counts	41
Invoice	42
Jazz	44
The Lyrebird	45
Walking Easter Sunset Down	46
Whitefaced Heron on the Bong Bong Flats	47
The Artist & His Model	48
I'd Like to Write a Poem	50
The News (Poetry Tells)	51
You Over There; Me, Here	55
A Beginner's Guide to Wabi-Sabi	57
Skipping the Rope	59
The Book of Daniel	60
The Sword & The Pen	61
Dog Sonnet	63
After a Long Drought	64
Sometimes, a Shallow Sea	65
Telling it Slant	66

Splitting Wood	67
Spring in Late Summer	69
The Reader	71
Night Lies	72
She & I	73
No Words	75
Welcome Swallows	78
The Art of Saturday	79
Colour Theory	80
The Child & Time	83
You Know How This Goes	88
The End of Poetry (As We Know It to Be)	91
Amen: A Moment of the World	92

Two—*Outside*

The World is Here for its Own Delight	97
Ubirr	98
Gaudeamus Igitur	100
Four Reservoir Tanka	101
Black Mountain Tanka	102
Lichen	103
Two Tanka for BL	104
Outside	105
We Are Not Finished at the Skin	109
Five Soft Nets	119
The Godwit Shores	122
Estuary	123
Dolphin Point	126
South Coast Sedoka	127
Among the Lighted Woods with Dante	128
Whitefaced Heron Above the Green Creek	129

Ghazal of the Weather Upon the Lake	130
Flood Tide	132
Flat Rock, September	133
Inland	137
The Hill Again	139
Hammock Hill Haiku	142
Up	143
Wait	145
The Hill	146
The Halflife of Coal	147
Revelation Days	152
Above the Snowies on the Day of First Snow	154
The Jetty	155
The Bay	158
Jimbaran Bay, Late October	160
At My Brother's House	161
Tropicbird	162
Spring Snow, Reno	163
Basin & Range	165
Grace	166
Fifty Words (or more) for Snow	167
Puck	168
The Wild Life of Southern Ontario	170
Ontario Slides	172
Inside Passage, Sunday Morning	174
Halfway Home	175
Rain at Eltham	177
Along the River Tonight	179

Three—In *Medias* Res

Doing the Numbers	183

January Poplars	185
Mecca	187
Balmain Nocturne	189
With Sarasvati Under the Lemon-Scented Gum Tonight	190
Blues Point Blues	191
The Cycles of the Moon	192
Yours Tonight	198
A Death in the Family	199
Flash Fiction	200
Three Shadows	201
Disappearance	202
The Last Day	203
Body Copy	205
In Medias Res	207
Catullus at Dusk, Lustful and Heartbroken, Tries His Hand at Haiku	209
Shreds	210
Youth: A Second Coming	212
Fish Me Up Plural	214

Four—Bach, Or Is It *Ravel?*

At Night the House	219
Bach, Or Is It Ravel?	220
Self-Portrait	221
Casting Shadows in Early April	222
Your Voice	223
Windfall	224
The Geography of the Middle Distance	225
So Little to Say	226
The Propinquity of Snow	227
November Rain	228
Landscape with Laptop	229

Five—Break & *Enter*

I Ran So Far	233
Among Trees	234
Fog Lies	236
One AM Sublime	238
Poem on Maundy Thursday	240
At Home on a Sunday Trying to Find Nothing to Do	242
April into May	245
Transit of Venus	252
What Happens if the Heart's Not Where Home Is	253
Break & Enter	255
Old Beginnings	257
Birthday Letter #51	259

Six—Why You're *Here*

The Peach Trees on Station Street	265
One Turning	267
Winter Comes in Overnight	268
The Moon is Round, and Fires Ring	269
Cicada Sonnet	270
Black Swan Moment	271
Comes a Time	272
Dark Moon Sestets	275
The Last Day of September	276
Nine Pines on Kangaloon	277
All the Campbelltowns	281
The Schoolhouse	283
The Teacher	284
A Memory of Fall	286

Spring	287
The Iris	289
Holding My Father's Heart	291
Arms & A Boy	294
The Nature of All Things	301
The Gardens of Beijing	304
The Love Song of the Forest & The Field	310
I am my Beloved's, & My Beloved is Mine	313
Imagine an Afternoon	315
Why You're Here	316
Drop Anchor	319

Epilogue

Page One	323

Notes

Notes	327

Foreword

Old Beginnings; or a Beginner's Guide to *A Beginner's Guide*

…the present is what your life is…
—Mary Oliver, "Mornings at Blackwater"

For sixty years I have been forgetful,
Every minute, but not for a second
Has this flowing toward me stopped or slowed.
—Jalal al-Din Rumi (tr. Coleman Barks), "The Music"

1.

WHEN I FIRST posted news of this book on Instagram, a good friend replied with a question: "A Beginner's Guide—to what? To Poetry?"

It's not really a guide to anything, I replied. It's a collection of poems, some recent, some from way back, and that's its title, which I take from one of the poems in it ("A Beginner's Guide to Wabi-Sabi").

But if the book is any kind of a guide, it's a guide to beginning. Beginning is what it's about—beginning again and again each time, as if each moment were a new world and a last chance and your life were a poem that wanted you to write it.

Which is to say: this collection gathers, around some loose themes, the poems I have written recently, sometimes not so recently—the poems that I have written and rewritten and kept. I guess there are many themes in these poems, almost as many as there are poems, each one being and recording a moment as new and wild as each moment is; but beginning is one theme that runs through them all.

2.
There is not one way to live. Your life is not prescribed; you make it up as you go. Each life is its own, to be fathomed and fashioned at the same time. A boat to be built as you sail it. And the truest beauty may be the deepest authenticity. A good life and a lucky one is a life begun as long as it lasts—a making of your way with wonder and curiosity, with discernment and finesse and forgiveness, a way made against tall odds, lived with as much hope and care and kindness and gratitude as you can remember how to practise. Well, that's the way I try to go about it, imperfectly, daily. And these poems record my failure.

"If you do with conviction the next and most necessary thing, you are always doing something meaningful and intended by fate." So wrote Jung in 1953 to someone who wanted to know what constituted a good life. There is no prescribed course, he said. The authentic life is the one lived moment by moment, taking the best course one can steer; by such means, open-minded, clear-headed, attempting always what seems right and true and helpful and generous and shapely, I would add, you are likely to go the way your soul hopes you will, and so you will keep coming true.

3.
There is an idea about that a book of poems, like a life, will cohere, congeal even, around a concept or a plot. But poems happen the way a life happens: you make them the way you make your way, as well as you can, in response to what you meet where life lands you. The best lives are enacted intuitions, adaptations to circumstance, navigations steered by love. Not by fashion or expectation or the dictates of the market or the fiat of another. The collections I love best go like that, too. They are curations of the best of what—the sense and the form—one has been able to make of what happened.

A good life is a beginning that goes on and on, getting better at doing what it alone can do, the more practice it gets, the wiser it grows through time. True change, I have often thought, is not how you become different, but how you grow more and more like who you, alone, are. And that's not a project you can perform in theory; it's a life you fashion in real time, the way a cricketer fashions an innings out in the middle, ball by ball.

4.

Two early poems in *A Beginner's Guide* strike the chords and dance the figures on which these poems might be said to improvise (though most of them did not know they were doing that when I wrote them).

In "Standing" I write—speaking of the shade three roughbarked apples (angophoras) throw across a meadow by a lake—*that* is "how I'd like to dwell/ my days—theirs the kind of trace/ I'd like to leave: a shifting/ Mark, downstream of every weather." And in "Jazz," speaking of poetry as if it were jazz, as if both were a metaphor, I conclude: "It's a life/ that makes you up as it goes down:/ No plan; just a fistful of chords/ and a lightness of touch and some bird song…/ An improv so tight someone must/ surely have scored it, but no one/ ever did. Or ever will again." "Standing" comes from 2020; "Jazz" from 2010. Ten years apart, each poem part of the same piece, though each was a beginning again, a starting fresh.

And from 2015, splitting those two poems like a log near the middle, is the poem "Why You're Here: In Case One Day You Need to Know," which says in so many words what many of the poems in this book of beginning imply: "You're here to learn/ To walk the way that only your feet can/ Teach you." And:

> You're here to divine
> The world a bit, to walk the god in you
> Out with you, to make your moment
> On earth worthy of the suffering it costs
> You. And those you love. And the earth.
> You're here to keep coming undone, to
> Keep opening, like an answer toward its
> Question…

5.
This is a book of beginning, then. Of living originally, as if each moment were the first morning, as if the dew were still on it and this, your first coffee. It isn't really a guide, of course. It's a book of poems, of instances, of beginning. Horace felt that a poem should delight and instruct. By "instruct" I'm pretty sure he didn't mean tell people how to lead their lives. Poetry is for witness, for seeing deep and saying fresh what has long been felt but rarely said. Because it demands vulnerability and honesty and integrity, poetry always models and may provokes a more careful consideration of how a life might be practised—with a little more humour or grace or tenderness or toughness, for instance. One might try to live one's days as if they were poems you were trying to write, as if life were a work of art you'd like to make good before you go: this may be the kind of instruction Horace thought a poem might perform. And I'd be with him.

    These poems are a celebration of wakefulness, of moments of world, an invitation always to begin. For to begin is to be; "'begin' is an anagram of 'being'". But don't worry: there's a fair bit of beginning but not a lot of guidance in this beginner's guide. There's quite a lot of noticing, though. And sadness. And delight.

6.
Each poem here tries to see something—in one's heart, in one's life, in the world, in others' lives, in the song of birds—originally, truthfully, and to get it said justly. Each poem here is an instance of being, a beginning. Some poems here are about keeping going when life is hard; others are about finding depth when life feels light; some are about the practice of making art (playing a piano again after thirty years, being Matisse, being a lake that goes dry for decades and then rises into lake-hood again overnight, making a poem). There are love poems here, too, poems for dogs and birds and places and children and weather and moments. Each is an enactment of (inevitably flawed and partial) wakefulness, of openness of heart and eye.

    But don't worry: you won't learn how to begin anything here. These are reminders a poet is giving himself about how important it is always to start and keep on starting. That ancient craft.

    One's own life is hard enough to understand and fashion freshly, moment by moment; your life is up to you.

7.
"The present is what your life is," writes Mary Oliver in "Mornings at Blackwater." The present is what your life is. Yes. This is another way of saying what these poems are trying to practise. Presence is what one's soul seems to want of you; it's what we need of each other, and it is the beginning of what the earth needs from us—to belong as well as one can to each moment of the world you are given.

    A remarkable number of Mary Oliver's poems happen in the morning. In the worst times of my life mornings have been the hardest moments to get through. So it was, I think, for Oliver. But morning—the phenomenon of morning in the world, and the practice of morning in a human life, of waking and beginning again daily—was her lifelong metaphor for presence. For turning up in your life and in the world, notwithstanding, and bearing witness and taking small good steps. I suppose these poems of mine, without very much awareness that is what they were trying to do, practise what Mary Oliver, and Henry Thoreau and many others, have preached.

    Looked at another way, this is a book of mornings, then. Not so much mornings as a subject (though there are some mornings among the moments here), but morning, dawning, beginning, as a way. *A Beginner's Guide* is a long aubade, regretful about what has already passed, about love lost, but stubbornly glad, as Jack Gilbert puts it, and determined to keep paying attention and living deliberately. Elegantly. Well. To make of one's life a world of mornings.

8.
To begin is to lay yourself open to what might come, without presumption; it is to be vulnerable. A good poem is a vulnerability made manifest and shapely—made habitable, durable. So is a good life. To be fully alive is to live beyond categories and nomenclature. To be a beginner is to stand on the edge of embarrassment and risk and delight and awe—prepared and expectant, but never too sure, never presumptuous. Cynicism and ideology preclude openness—the schooled innocence, the profound attention, of the beginner. Love made wise by form and care: this is the way of beginning. We live in an era of stereotypes and categories; poetry is how we refuse to conform. Beginning is what poetry insists on.

9.
Presence, the art these poems essay, is hard work, and I know that in many of the moments these poems record, I was halfway absent.

But still they reached me. "For sixty years," Rumi wrote, "I have been forgetful." Me, too. But the world is not forgetful. The trick seems to be to stay open—to what the world is always offering, whether or not we have the sense to notice. Or at least, to be attentive enough to language to let it trawl into awareness most of what you missed at the time. This is what I think I'm talking about in my poem "The World is Here for Its Own Delight":

My mind today has no account to make
    Of joy. In this it fails the world. And lets
My body down, which wants the day to have
    Her way with it. Later the light and the water
Low in the dam and the flowers that spike on gums
    High on the scarp and the heron that overflies me
As I take the pass south... these fingerprints
    The real world wants to leave on me, imprint,
Anyway, on a speeding mind that knows
    Too little sense to feel them when they land.

One has a partner in this work of apprehension: the world is more than half of it (and of our being in the world). Being—in a way that's useful for the world beyond one's mere self—is a kind of being-with. One's self is not reducible to one's mind or mood or biography or self-story. Perhaps, as William James would have it, the Self is a community—of all that one's affection reaches out to, of all that reaches you, in your self-absorption. The moments leave fingerprints if you let them.

10.

Presence takes a lifetime to learn. It takes an eternity to arrive in each moment wide awake. To live as a beginner you serve a long apprenticeship, and I've been at it sixty years, and see how far short I fall. Hokusai, the great Japanese landscape painter, whose work influenced the way the impressionists and many others taught themselves to see, painted the work for which he is best known, "The Great Wave at Kanagawa" when he was seventy. And he wrote: "Until the age of seventy, nothing I drew was worthy of notice… When I reach eighty, I hope to have made some progress, and at ninety to see further into the underlying principles of things, so that at one hundred years I will have achieved a divine state in my art, and at 110 every dot and every stroke will be as though alive."

It takes a long time, then, to arrive in the present moment, ready for it, awake to it and what it requires and some of what it yields. A life, like a work of art, is a practice at which you will fall short most of the time, but at which you will get better if you keep turning up. All living, and all art, entail a falling short: this Hokusai believed; it is *how* we fail (with what devotion and hope), in other words, not so much in how perfectly we achieve the witness, or take "the next and most necessary step" that counts. There is an idea in Japanese culture that a degree of hand-madeness, of imperfection, makes a face, a life, a work of art, most beautiful. I have that idea in mind in the poem from which this collection draws its title: "A Beginner's Guide to Wabi-Sabi," and Hokusai has it in mind in his words above. We never, in other words, arrive, and what falls short is part of how a work or a life achieves itself.

I find myself at sixty deeply drawn to another idea that prevailed in Hokusai's time: one starts a new cycle of life at sixty—one in which, if you've continued to serve that long apprenticeship in living, you might begin at last to make some progress. Toward beginning.

11.
These are times infatuated with newness; some see these as end days, and the past as a failed enterprise. These are times intolerant of many things, mostly old things, including especially the idea of craft and the idea of slowness and devotion. I am already old and out of step with fashion. The beginnings I have in mind are profoundly respectful of oldness and perpetuity—and of crafts it takes time and attention and humility to learn. The beginning we need now is the kind we always did—the kind poetry practises, a kind of presence it takes a while to learn. It is the kind of beginning you perform in your heart and mind and life daily, a molecular revolution you wake to each morning—a refusal of cant and platitude, a commitment to do justice to the world and everyone and every moment we encounter in it.

So let this book be a beginning of that old sort.

What we need is more of what poetry practises: small, uncompromisingly truthful and kind gestures, vernacular and authentic and always human. And please, you young and Messianic ones, keep Hokusai's words in mind and beware the certainties of youth and the ruthlessness of piety and iconoclasm. And take your time while you still have it.

12.
Beginning, then, is the oldest trick in the world; true beginnings may be the oldest; they've been a long time coming. What's old about good beginnings, what is past about presence, may be this: the readiness one slowly learns, the tolerance, the humility and acuity. The oldness of good beginnings is what you have learned from missteps and bad luck and good grace and heartbreak and devotion to the craft of staying the course and waking again the next day and getting after it a little better than the day before. It's the experience you bring to the innocence of your being with the world.

13.
As I close these thoughts on beginning, I hear a story on the car radio about a collection of the songs of endangered birds that has flown to the top five of the ARIA (Australian Record Industry Association) charts, putting Mariah Carey and the lugubrious Adele in the shade this Christmas. The songbirds are the original artists, nature's poets, the lyricists of the beginning of time. And each of the birds on the album is a bird—among them, the gang gangs, the red goshawk, the golden bowerbird, and the night parrot—endangered or extinct, by virtue of human occupation of the earth. *Songs of Disappearance* is the beautiful name of the album, which plays as I write now.

Poetry, it strikes me, is to human culture what birdsong is to nature. On the face of it inessential, like love. In how tenuously and tenaciously both birdsong and poetry hold on, they sing the peril and holiness of the earth. And of all lives upon it.

May these songs of beginning, then, remind us that we are living through a time of endings. For we are, the scientists tell us, inhabiting already a mass extinction event, and already much of what had animated our being on the earth is diminished or dying back or lost to us for good. Poetry, even passionate attention to what is left, feel like flimsy strategies against catastrophe. But without them we are all truly lost. We will have forgotten why we came and what it is that we live: our presence, our note or two in the lyric of this moment of existence. May we begin again at last to recall the beauty we lay waste to—in our lives and in our places—by the profligacy and violent neglect with which we occupy our lives and this earth. May we find in the bird songs and the poetry of lives begun again each moment the radical reimagining that may begin the salvation of this canticle of a spinning earth.

14.
May we not have left our beginning too late.

Prologue

Standing

THE WAY the trees, three
                rough-barked apples, throw their shade
  Across the grass through afternoon
Toward the saltmarsh and the dark bright water
                      of the lake is how I'd like to dwell

My days—theirs the kind of trace
                I'd like to leave: a shifting
  Mark, downstream of every weather,
A sometime recollection of how one learned,
                  at last, to stand in the light of the world.

I—Last *Things* First

An Old Lament

For Don O'Brien

MY FRIEND HAS passed. He's not the first,   but why are all the good folks
    Dying back, while rapists   and the pious thrive? An old lament
I share with the dogs and late winter   along the broken creek.

Several Birds & A Dog

IN TIME, one's children, like one's youth,   fly, but let no one rush them.
    Above the reservoir,   where I go for breathing lessons, smoke
Hawk circles, like a carpenter's hands,   sanding the east wind smooth.

THE DOG, who's learning this place   like a faith I'd like to practise,
    Abandons the made way   for the water's edge, the sedge and mud.
Among all that eludes him: firetail and treecreeper and wren.

Before the Day

For Jidi Majia

1.

BEFORE THE DAY has quite put on its clothes,
    I stand and watch an egret—cut, it seems,
From card—arrive upon the waking waters
    And put down. This is the edge a poem
Walks; this is the hour. Black against
    The monochrome swill of dawn, before the stream's
Unearthed the ore that is the wealth of winter
    Light, the white bird stands in saltmarsh shallows
To fish for day. And this is how the past
    Might wish it looked. The bird is how it was:

2.
Avid, like anyone else for breakfast, handsome
    In its need. And now the tide of day leaks in,
An amber swell among the callow pines,
    And the butcherbird arrives, trailing the single
Phrase he's made his own from all the book
    Of songs, to find the single page in the book
Of clouds—upon the table upon the deck—
    Where the weather of her day might be described.
Bronzewing begins her baleful swoon and soon
    The water's edge is dark, the egret bright,

3.
The morning a shorebird's flight to afternoon.
    My river is small, my years grow long. Two thousand
Years ago, amid the ceaseless war
    Of spring with fall, a poet walked, downcast
Into a river of lament. And once,
    A guest, I visited the town—our landing thrummed
On drums of war—where the body of the poet
    Of the river washed unremarked ashore.
But they seem to want to raise him now—these water
    Birds: the cormorant, the pelican,

4.
The swan. They crowd the shallows and sound their cries
    Like canon across the blue meniscus of dawn.
Of course, it may not be the fallen light
    Of last night's moon, the songs of the south, the heron's
Hymns—it may not be the broken heart
    Of poetry, it may not be these lines
I cast in memory—the river birds
    Trawl the morning waters to divine.
But they divine it anyway, these ava-
    Tars of hope, these engineers of grace.

5.
Another poet says: catastrophe
    Will find you, come what may, disgrace and grief;
The treachery of time will trip you up,
    And you will fail love, or love fail you.
Your work will be ignored, your name misspelled.
    The forests will likely fall, the libraries burn.
But something holds, and even in your wreck
    It holds you, too: the principle of love
Embodied in the bird that flares the dawn
    And thrives where you, your heart a rock, would sink.

6.
Perhaps it's true that in the way of things,
    One gets another life as what one loved
Best. To finish the work one left undone.
    Is Qu Yuan the butcherbird, perhaps—
His call a lamentation, his eyes a crime
    Against banality and sloth—that's sat
The arm of the chair on the deck, these hours now
    While I've rowed back along the poet's river
Where I journeyed six months ago in a dragon boat—
    The river where he sang and loved and sank?

7.
We live downriver from the past; we fish
    Our phrases from the stream. They are not ours.
We finish stanzas long ago begun;
    We fly them like a flock of migrant birds
Into the years. First days of spring on Erowal
    Could be the end of autumn in Hunan.
The truth, like earth, is round and liminal:
    The egret holds its shores. And all that's awake
In one's work and new in one's heart is an older longing
    Unfulfilled and drowned before its time.

8.
Behind the beach where my river recites its sea,
    The grasses are a brush in the hand of the wind,
And the dunes in the dawn are cold and pale as sleep—
    As an egret in the afternoon. And the script
These limber stems—these fervid dervish strands—
    Lay down may be the archetype of song:
A record of the plangency of being
    Once, and only once, alive in time.
So, if these sand dunes aren't old Qu Yuan,
    Then let them, please, and just this once, be me.

What Counts

1.

IN the qualitative world,
It's only quality that counts.

2.
This is the qualitative world.

3.
I'm counting on it.

Invoice

For Zdravka Evtimova

IF ONLY EACH poem were
    An invoice, as easily earned,
As quickly drawn and sent.
    If only it yielded so fast.

A poem that outlives you,
    A better thing than your life,
Pays at best one fifth of each
    Week's rent, one tenth of

The maintenance. Which madman
    Dreamed up economics? But still
You write. For you cannot
    Find a way to stop. There is

Nothing else you know how
    To do. Each letter of a poem's
Alphabet knows more places,
    Tells more faces, than you will

Meet in a life, each phrase holds
    Your hand as if it were a child's.
A line can shine a constellation
    Down; a line can spare a life. For these

Five poems I wrung from years
    And plucked from gardens where
Numerals hung like fruit, the world
    Will pay one hundred dollars, the cost

Of another parking ticket in the
    City. But look: it has, this invoice,
Bloomed these lines, which I give
    To you like peaches ripe with June.

Jazz; or, Every Poem is a Love Song, Really

P<small>OETRY</small>, like jazz, works best
    too late and in the dark. Poetry
sounds like jazz feels—heartbreak
        shrugged off at daybreak and reprised
in the sad amplitude of dusk.
    Poetry's emotion enjambed and

played into thought and
    surrendered into imagery stolen,
like black notes, from the secret
        lives of others—its lyrics leased
from everyone who ever felt
    how hard it is to live on,

Sometimes, in the sorrow-
    ful beauty of it all, but never
could find the key or walk
        the complicated rhythm
from the top. It's a life
    that makes you up as it goes down:

No plan; just a fistful of chords
    and a lightness of touch and some bird
song. It's a rehearsal undressed,
        an improv so tight someone must
surely have scored it, but no one
    ever did. Or ever will again.

The Lyrebird

For Debbie Lim

WRITING is hard work all morning long—
                                     as if I were on trial for each phrase.
    Sentenced half to death by two o'clock,
I leave the house and take the driving-too-fast meditation
                                     all the way to the village. Along the Mt Scanzi Road

I panic a lyrebird from its sonic camouflage. Pretence will get you
    Nowhere fast. I drive a little slower home, where, later,
                                     writing proves just as hard in the dark.
Boobook at midnight: if two syllables are all you have, you'd better make them pay.

Walking Easter Sunday Down

W E'RE OUT WALKING Easter Sunday
                back down to earth—the little ones, the dog,
And you and I—all along the river. It's early April, and the afternoon feels
Somewhat overwrought—
                all that chocolate, one supposes; all that premature triumph over death—

    And the sky's disguised as the inside of an abalone shell. A late Indian summer is
Transposed tonight into something
                more like what April's meant to be—that cruel and beautiful month—
                        in ordinary times like these.
    Sunset over flooded fields is opalised bone exhumed, a brilliant line
                of broken thought that fades
                        the moment you think it.

Whitefaced Heron on the Bong Bong Flats

I F I WERE painting this
                        I'd leave it pretty much alone.
   The clouds engvorged and urgent as love,
The flats thatched with summer; the river, as ever, silty and recalcitrant
    And low. The things in their places
                                 compose themselves after a fashion
No fashion can touch. But this looks about right to me.
   Or, perhaps I'd daub some purple down the bottom right hand corner—

Just where the heron works
                         the drainage ditch, her bill, she hopes, as sharp
   As her hunger—just to counterpoint the cloud. (And pin it down.)
The body of the bird, a rhetorical question, is the colour of the rain
    That swarms the coming storm, snagged
                                   in the dusk on the mountain; her eponymous
Face is where the sun burns through. But how will I treat the rain,
   Which hazes us now, and grazes the bird,
                                         a study toward the larger work that's coming?

The Artist & His Model

After Henri Matisse's "The Artist and His Model"

EACH THING on earth shapes the only
        Question it knows how shape—
The question only it knows how to ask,
        And only you. Each earthly thing poses its self:

The heron, a patient bolt of lightning running slant
        Above the river flats, for instance; the breaking
Wave and the tern that drops—a bow become
        An arrow—hard into the backwash;

The sheoaks eschewing all ceremony and colour
        In an onshore breeze, and the contingent
Geology of the dunes the oaks keep faith with; closer
        To home, the windflower I picked this morning, walking,

And later held in my left hand and drew with my right,
        A chaste little odalisque, in the room, while you slept;
The curtains parted now by a yellow afternoon
        Wind; the goldfish swimming, in their bowl,

A lyric recollection of your hands, which you held
        Near as bait to the fish earlier, a school of fingers
Teaching your fast mind to slow; the chair
        That waits for you in its striped pyjamas;

And, ah, now the chair with you in it again.
        And if I pull my stool close to you, it's not
To crowd, but to gate-crash politely
        The querulous ecology of your embodied self.

The tilt of your shoulder is the shape
        My mind assumes, resting there; your breasts—
The last fruit (persimmons, let's say) on the last tree—
        Seem to want me to name the many dialects

Of disappointment and delight. Your body, a lazy phrase
        Or two displayed across my couch, makes a bed, if not a bed-
Fellow, of my mind, in which I wake late, the taste of fire
        Still blue on my tongue. Every piece of the carnal world

Takes the shape of a question it alone knows
        How to pose. And you can keep on posing
Yours as long as you like, for I am in no hurry
        To make an answer; I'm content just to follow my hand

As it makes these lines, which look for you
        And trace the way my mind is made over
But never made up, swallowing hunger, and touching
        And touching in violet silences the skin
Of so many haptic and haphazard questions.

I'd Like to Write a Poem

I'D LIKE to write a poem as still
   As the afternoon has fallen,
                    the heat gone from it now, and rain
Coming down from the north.
                     I'd like it to breathe, this poem,

   With just such nervous ease as the air
Above these river flats breathes tonight
                at twenty-seven minutes after six;
                        and I wish it would stir—this poem
   I make for you—under its skin, inside its clothes,
                  the way you once stirred,
                          waiting for me.

The News (Poetry Tells)

*It is difficult to get the news from poems,
yet men die miserably every day
for lack of what is found there.*

—William Carlos Williams, "Asphodel, That Green Flower"

1.

THE NEWS poetry tells
Is that everyone suffers
        Like this; everyone delights,
Periodically, like this, remembers what they'd like to forget, forgets
        The sunlight in the voice
            Of the finch—all those
Fibre-optic ligatures, which bind the wound
        That never wants to heal and carry news of us to the world:
        That is the news, and poetry tells it,
            The way the finches do.

2.
Inside the sometime misery
Of things, the engines of death,
The masques of sex, the comings
And comings again of age, the mystic machinery of weather, the lie
Of the land, a coherence
Holds, an impossibly beautiful
Grammar. There's a music that fashions the world,
Moment by moment. A music that's always just finished—but a touch,
A chord, a line, now and then,
Seems to recall how

3.
Some of it went
And carries it home
And dresses it in silence again.
Poetry delivers the news the way a cat brings you a trophy in her mouth,
This mouse that used to
Have a head, say, and lays it at
Your feet. And wants milk. The news is that nothing is
New, and that everything is new again each time it's deeply felt
And spoken thick and slant; the news is,
That, by the way, you can stop

4.
    Wanting now and again: Heaven's
Been here a long time,
        Waiting; you've probably been looking
Too far out. Poetry reads the book the rivers wring from the valleys.
    Poetry writes the prayers the days say
        To the weeks that pass without
A word from her. But inside the book of songs
    That poetry hums, inside the order it overhears and refashions
        In voluble clay, lies also what the order is not—
            The possibility anything else might

5.
    Have happened and might yet,
At just about any moment,
        But generally doesn't. Poetry, like country,
Contains the chaos it cures; it tells the devil in the detail. It finds Eros
    In the Weeties pack and offers you
        A taste. For every immaculate pattern
Wants to unpick itself and will find a way and a day,
    And it must, or the circle will slow and the music
        Will stop. This is the news, which you knew all along,
            And poetry tells it again.

6.
And again. It is the rhythm inside
The pain, the music inside
The intelligence of every thing, the echo
Of her lovely cry, the architecture of your resplendent despair,
The plangent beatitudes of love
In all its raucous denominations: everything is
An image of the truth; everything, even the worst thing,
Is how a small phrase of the music plays, and you, too,
In the face of the false witness of the mirror
In your mind, are part,

7.
A very small part, of a very old
Tune, the sex and death, the feather
Under the breath of the god, of it all.
Poetry tells the big story small, the old story new and lets you bear it.
Poetry is an echo of your questions
Come back to you, more neatly put
Than you could manage in the dark. Poetry rings its small bell
Inside the crowded temple,
Where the money has never stopped
Changing hands.

You Over There, Me Here:
A Whodunit in Three Sestets

1.

MEANTIME, where I am, the sun is out
                and the day can't get enough of it;
  She sprawls like a coven of working girls, perfect and sure of it, nipples
Like rose buds, in the garden beds of this paradise
                I'm lost in. Meantime, five or six cicadas, summer's early adopters,
  Are over-achieving in the outstretched arms of mid-afternoon.
All our stories of belonging start somewhere else, you say. Well, sure.
                                    And what's left of them
  End up here. In an exquisite mess on the floor of my studio.
                          Some old moments are rehearsing even now

2.

In demi-hemi-semiquavers on the silver tongues
                      of the leaves of the water poplars by my door,
  And memory streams in blue and unsteady from the east
                            to tease them apart. There was a big bang—
That's all I remember. Oh, and then she kissed me;
                you can make up the rest. Look, I have no narrative in me;
  I have no story to tell, and no story to tell me otherwise.
                      I have galaxies of words. Congealed voices,
Orbiting, elliptical around a thousand original suns. And I hear these riffs,
  These chords and notes, arpeggios of archetypal weather.
                          But if there was a plot, I lost it long ago.

3.
You don't like cicadas, you say;
                                    but I don't hear them giving much of a damn
    About that. The lizard loose on what's left of winter's woodpile
Is keeping his tail to himself. Every story starts
                                            in the middle of someone else's wood.
    Pieces of it, anyway. Some dark, some light. Meanwhile you're over there,
Falling out of yourself into the arms of a new city. While, here, the frogs pick up,
    In the dark, stitches the cicadas dropped in the dusk:
                                      dot points in search of a sentence; partners
                                                                in need of a crime.

A Beginner's Guide to Wabi-Sabi

Nearly fifty-five years I've been bluffing
                    my way toward imperfection,
             and look:
    Here I am, and not a moment too soon. Heaven's not getting any
Younger, and earth's the same old broken vessel
    It's been since they threw it.
                              And dropped it. And the innumerate gulls
Brawl and heckle along the tideline in their silver dealers' jackets,
    As if the afternoon were an enterprise
                                with decent midrange prospects.

The day's been making its mind up
                            all day, and now it's decided against it.
    Rain draws the curtains back in a wide circle all about us.
We're cured, it seems, and free
      To go. But we stand on the beach
                           in the baffled light, and we're not alone,
And the afternoon's tide is going out, taking a thousand beachgoers slowly home
    With it. The beach goes on without us, though—
                                    the surf choppy and irascible.

If beauty is truth, no one's telling it straight,
                                 and no one ought to try.
   The better you get, the worse it looks; a self-fulfilling prophecy
The sea's been declaiming since the world first got wet.
   Behind the beach, in the sky's lower left margin,
                                 the scarp is scrawling edits
On the proofs of *A Beginner's Guide to Wabi-Sabi*, a book it's been ruining
   200 million years or more. Writing and rewriting,
                   disdainful of the fleeting orthodoxies,
                                     the massive condescension, of the clouds.

Each year everything, including hope, grows smaller
                          and much more like itself: erosion,
   It seems, is the way to go, until you're gone for good.
My coffee's gone cold, but it's still coffee, all the way down
   To the bottom, and the children have done
                          teasing anemones and wandered off
Along the creek. One can carry imperfection too far, of course,
   And that's what I did yesterday,
                  all the way there and back again
                                in the wrong shoes entirely—

Two miles, at least, too far.
             Straining after fitness and purpose, when a smarter man
   Would have let them find him at their own pace,
And now I limp after the little ones in the dusk
   Like Achilles into battle. Here, take my hand, love;
                            take my crazed and weathered hand.
Lean into me and let's stumble out of nothingness—or into it; it's hard to say. Let's follow
   The children, inventing their lives all over again in the grey light;
                          let's see if we can walk
                              some crooked sense into the sand.

Skipping the Rope

For Lucy

JUST THIS, then: a girl in blue pajamas—
    Her small legs crossed at the ankles,
Her bare feet re-arranging winter
    Into arabesques on the kitchen floor,
And she turns a rope, finer than spider's
    Web, over (and over) her head, and jumps,
As it sweeps, like nothing at all, the floor
    Boards clean beneath her feet. She lifts off
Twice between rotations, chanting some
    Absent-minded rhyming fairy banter,
Rehearsing at light-speed who she is, becoming
    The world's most nimble feather
Weight, the prettiest boxer there ever
    Will be, while she waits for her toast to rise.

The Book of Daniel

For Daniel

Y OU HAVE the gift of understanding dreams,
    And this pride of lions rests in the den of your heart.
You are the dream of peace they sleep, it seems,
    So, sleep, and know your self and find your part.

You have the gift of calming troubled kings
    By telling them the truth in what they see.
Sad men will rain bad dreams upon all things,
    So, sing, and wake the world and let it be.

You have the gift of making exile home.
    You have the gift of being where you stand.
Home won't always be this bay you're from,
    So, stay, and love the ground on which you land.

So then, sleep and dream and know and sing and stay.
We have the gift of you. Let this be your day.

The Sword & The Pen

For Daniel

So, HAVE you been doing much
Sword-fighting lately? The boy

Asks because, you know, fathers live
Forever and have seen the history

Of the world enacted around them,
And most of it they had a hand in,

The piracy and dragon-slaying,
In particular. There is not a thing

They do not know or have not done.
Not much, I say. I'm getting a little

Rusty. This is an unhelpful response.

He's holding it: a scythe, a foundered
Tool. An artifact he's dug from his mother's

Vegetable patch. A new moon already old.
It's for sword-fighting, isn't it? He insists,

More interested in metal than metaphor.
A child, like most children, taut

With the concrete poems of which
They know the real world is really made.

Do you think that's why it's so rough?

Later we fight. He uses the rasp we use
To keep the edges of the kitchen knives

Keen. And because, as he well knows,
The present belongs to him, he wins.

He repels my slow and antiquated thrusts
And stabs me twice. Once to finish me

Off. A second time to start me up again.
To die again another day.

Dog Sonnet

For Honey, when she was young

So MY DOG, that sheep, sneaks inside in her wolf's clothing, her
    Hired fur, when I carry the cinders out to the yard, and she lies

On the floor in her browns and whites, and she looks up furtively
    When I come back in, as if she'd rather not be recognised from the TV

Series every child watched in black and white back when the world
    Was not yet too much for us. With pious, world-weary poise,

She folds her paws in their long white socks, and she rests
    Her long head there, as if in prayer. But in truth, she's making

Herself a small target; she's trying to disappear inside her own half-
    Hearted, full-pedigreed disguise. And that strategy lasts

Ten seconds at least, for the house is a carnival of discarded things,
    And she knows she's borrowed half her time already. My mind,

I think, is like that, too: filling every silence it fakes; putting some
    Smart move on every bright idea that wanders halfway into view.

After a Long Drought

LATE AFTERNOON is caught
                in its own headlamps, astonished
  At the cool ambition of the light; the lake stands beside the road, painting
Herself in watercolours, the way she used to run:
                            cloud shadows still wet in the middle

    Distance a week after rain. Meantime, nothing's changed
The mind of the Cullarin Range,
                      which sits gravely by, straight-backed
  And dry-eyed, arranging your obit all over again
                              in charcoal and deadfall
                                      and all this born-again weather.

Sometimes, A Shallow Sea

For Kate Lines

H OW DOES it feel to be the oldest living lake on the earth—
   And most days not so much a lake as a paddock where a drought
Has broken out—and then overnight, sometimes, a shallow sea?

Telling It Slant

I SIT THIS once with my back to the world.
                           An afternoon in summer,
    French doors flung wide. I cross my legs in the red kitchen-chair,
And the shower that drums the awning behind
                                could be the rat that tap-

Danced the ceiling last night, the ceiling beneath which we lay.
                                      The rat that's been practising up there
    Since Christmas. Meaning comes the way it wants to come, and when; one thing
Dressed up slyly as another.
                      No one's asking you to like it.
                                       But it pays to start joining
                                                   some dots.

Splitting Wood

Enemies—
Part of a world
Nobody seemed able to explain
But that had to be
Put up with.
—Seamus Heaney, "A Herbal"

S PLITTING WOOD, I think of my enemy.
    It seems to me a useful kind of striking
Back, feeding, as it does, fire with a better
    Kind of fire: it's an upcycling of lost limbs, a judo
Of redemptive violence, and it leaves no one
    Very much the worse
               for wear. I raise the splitter
High and swing it low, baffled by the poverty
    Of my enemy's soul, so very like my own,
Sorry to have been the cause of such banality
    Of thought and word, but very, very certain

              Of my aim: not *at* the log,
    But *through* it. And when this afternoon—
Thinking of the head, in particular, of the one
    Who's chosen me as his work, and libel
As his play—
        when this afternoon
               I brought my splitter

    Down, and brought it down hard, on what
I'd thought would be the toughest round
    Of all, it split like a pumpkin and spilled a million
Termite larvae, pale unleavened angels, across
    The rainy and all-hallowed end of day.

Spring in Late Summer

WELL, IT TURNED out what I'd thought a new spring
    Risen in the yard was only a broken pipe,

And the pool—fringed with grasses as green as all
    Kentucky, visited not only by the whitefaced heron

And the wren and the many pied and tawny
    Birds, but also by the tiger snake, which curled

On the soft grey body of the mud and cooled
    In the blue-eyed shadows till my daughter, chasing

A ball, frightened her, and next day, visited, like
    The doctor, by a copperhead, and who knows how

Many makes of other snakes on other days,
    For word of this sudden oasis had spread like fire

Through the hottest summer days in years—that fabled
    Pool, it transpires, was an extravagant water bill

And the work of half a day for our friend the plumber
    To mend.
              And now the mud has baked hard in summer's

Cooling furnace until it is a tessellated
    Concrete shelf you could turn your ankle on. Undine

Has dwindled into her undone poet's remains, and the phrases
    Of the underground love they make are fuller yet

Of the idiom of the dead, and they clatter, those deathless words,
    At dusk, like stones thrown to wake the living and break

The windows we make to keep the real world safely out.

The Reader

He sits a wicker chair reading
Poems in the sun, shaking his head
And looking up, as if he remembers

All this. As if everything had come
Clear now.
              The midafternoon traffic
Gets busy along the road. It's late

Winter, and the air is dry. The light
Has pinned itself up in the tallness
Of the trees, and it hangs there,

Full of itself, and blossoms stand and
Fan their pale faces along the narrow
Avenues of the plum.
                        But he notices

None of this. He rises and steps
Away and the moment goes on
Without him.
              At the door, he turns

And sees the cat wound tight
Beneath the chair he's left:
The shadow of his reading

Self reading on a while longer.

Night Lies: An Aubade

Night lies outside like
  A dog that wants to come in—
The moon is its bowl.

I FALL asleep with Amy Lowell and wake with Jay Parini and some lines about poetry: Poems are for making emptiness out of crowdedness. Space out of clamour. Silence under fire. A poem is sacred geography—a holy place and an enchanted chart of the way there. But not back again. A poem is an unkempt secret. Some god's dislodged longing. It comes from deep outside yourself and takes you nowhere near where you thought it would. Writing one you let that self older than your self love the words it loves and speak them without asking questions first. Like what on earth they think they mean. And so this late winter morning I know that when

The first white blossoms
  Go off like soft bombs along
Plumtree limbs—it's you.

She & I

TODAY, AS I drove the pastured floodplains home, quartered
   By a cold abortive morning in the family court,
I drew off the highway, baffled at my body's insistence
   On itself in the midst of the just, uncivil war of thought
And sense my head had mistaken for myself.
                               On his walk
   To the gallows, the condemned man steps around the puddle
Of overnight rain; the man losing hope of knowing himself
   A father again still finds the wit and will to stop
And walk a bush track and take a pee.
                            I nodded embarrassed
   Greeting to another soul parked in his privacy
There, and in slow motion I vaulted the gate that keeps
   The traffic from the scrub, and I saw on the trail that walked
The distance farther off into a fluted dark
   Among tall trees, a whitefaced heron, and she saw me.
We held each other a moment in quiet disregard,
   Her body a mute grey question mark to which
The katabatic breeze,
                 which fell from the scarp and ran
   The turpentines my way like a child, spoke
The answer in her mother's tongue.
                          And still, she stood,
   When I returned, a little off the trail, spiking
The reeds where the race memory of a creekbed
   Crawled, a one-fingered typist inordinately proud
Of the one word she knew how to spell. The body

    Of the world, I thought, is the solid form
Of that Babel of languages in which forever
    Speaks its truths, or keeps its peace, depending on
The way a moment wants to feel.
                                 We stood, she
    And I, a minute then, and perhaps if one of us
Had cigarettes, we might have shared a few.
                                           Instead,
    We shared the silence language dreams of being,
hope the hardest word of it to hear.

No Words

*T*HERE ARE NO *words*
at first. At first light,

    instead, a clangour
of thoughts, which pass

    through the end of sleep
like empty goods trains

    and shout dawn down and
try to drown morning

    at birth. They carry you
everywhere but where

    you are and who you
always were. Waking

    will not always be
like this.   Start now;

    let the trains pass; hear
the bellbirds make the

    sunlit morning round. Bring
your mind nearer. Sit

    in the chair, let sunlight
curl in your lap; drink

    coffee and let things stand
as they are. Be among them.

    Sheoaks, shadows stilled,
stand the steep hills in which

    the town is set.
                      Come closer
in. Peach trees flower by the

    shed, and the morning clears
the kitchen of the mess

    your children made with
you last night, and you

    left like pieces of them
to care for when they'd

    gone.
          Nearer still. The woman
you love wakes among ash

    and mountain air a thousand
miles south, as close to you again

    as your fingers to the keyboard,
and your words are your lips,

   a quiet clatter on her skin. And
the scent of the potato vine

   that strings the paling
fence is a walk by the Seine

   in the rain that fell as light
all summer long.
                     There are

   no words at first. And then
there are words that were

   always here. Each word
is a bird—a spinebill, a sparrow,

   a gang gang, a hawk.
                     Say each
and fly, back into all the love

   you thought you'd lost—
the lust, the dust, the vast

   ness of what is—that never
wasn't yours. Call it *this*;

   become the words the day
would write. Begin:

   At first there are no words.

Welcome Swallows

I LOOK UP and there's rain on the window
    Like spilled glue, and the sun's still stuck in the sky.

    I look up again and there's the blue heron,
    That dandy, flying slantwise home on his tipsy

Toes, in the drunken teeth of the gale. Which
    Suddenly loses patience with poetry and me

    And shoulders open my door to carry
    Its animus inside, my anima out. But impatience

Is a lesson you only have to learn once, so I herd
    The weather out and welcome the swallows home

    And sit to practise at my desk what they've been
    Making in my roof by rote: mouthful after mouthful

Of world. Emptying the present tense out; bedding
    The future down. Making nothing happen. Just so.

The Art of Saturday

For Henry

SATURDAY morning. The kind
    Childhoods are meant to be

    Made of. The boy sees
The first bees of spring

In the daphne and the cherry.
    He goes inside and takes some

    Letterhead and writes on it
In crayon and comes back out

And posts a notice on the front
    Door: *welcome home bees oxox.*

Colour Theory; or, the End of the Line

His poems don't so much conclude as arrive.
—Dan Chiasson on Carl Phillips

For Robert Gray & for Lucy

THE MORNING has the look
     of a bride determined none of this
Will ever end; every sentence, she knows, has a life
Whose light will go out,
But not today. The morning is the future
Resting easy on the past, and *this is all*
         there is, it wants to tell you,
Rising on one elbow to kiss you on the mouth,
For now. Over breakfast, I sit,
        younger than I've been in years, reading
The New Yorker, where the critics sometimes write
As if their words had other lives
      and lived them,
And here's Dan Chiasson
Writing any number of the articles
Of one's own recalcitrant faith—
     poets work primarily in lines, he reminds
Me, *dissecting sentences,*
     scattering little cliffhangers
Across…a jagged terrain. It's Carl Phillips's terrain,
Specifically, he's mapping out: his hunger, which is one's own,
"To give shapelessness a form"—a thing

We do sometimes in sex, in art, in prayer, in pajamas, in deftly disarticulated
Choreographies of sense.
And because this has all at once become
A conversation that's earned us both a second
                                      coffee, I rise, inspired, to make it,
And the phone rings, and it's Robert Gray on the end
Of the line. Gray, painter among poets,
                                    each sentence a gesture
In charcoal first, each word a pot of exotic ink, each phrase
A careful assemblage of unexpected tertiaries
And elegant similes for light; it's Gray
This man of plainly spoken colours, his call enjambing
                                    abruptly all thought of coffee and stranding Phillips
There on the New York page.
 We talk a while,
Gray and I—the prose that comes fast; the poems
That drag their feet toward their death
Defying feat: (the transfiguration of the everyday,
                                    transubstantiation of the real). Pound,
He tells me (Robert always has a story like this)—Pound,
Who wanted us so desperately
                              to *keep* It, but to keep on *making* It
New—Pound once sued
His publishers for stepping
                down just the right line
In just the wrong place, and lost. We talk of Judy Beveridge
And Stephen Edgar, and how nothing is too bleak
For poetry to take on and turn back
The way it came—toward its other life as a model, for instance,
For a Pre-Raphaelite portrait of this very morning's bride,
Lost in thought somewhere

                          a long time ago, along a Canongate wynd…
So, when I put down the phone and return to New York,
There's Carl Phillips, where I left him, walking off every map on Dan Chiasson's page,
Quietly refusing even now to be anyone
                                    else's Famous Black and White Idea
Of who he is. Being instead, every other semitone
Of his unsettled sense of self.
And this, I see, is more, this morning,
                              than some pretty postmodern
Conceit: for my daughter, while my back was turned,
Has had the textas out, and she's turned the line
Drawing on page 22 of Carl Phillips, that cartographer of all our hearts'
False starts, into a Pop Art icon. And the poet's purple brows
And the neon yellow of his eyes
                  look more or less astonished
                                    in the cool antipodean light
At this his own quite sudden fifteen minutes
Of fame.

The Child & Time

For Henry

I

When I sit these days—
Or walk—
And wait for a poem
Mostly it's a child that comes.
Saying, for instance,
Just past the rabbit in her sorry cage,
The convolvulus and the white roses,
I carry you?
Putting words in my mouth
And offering up the burden of himself in response.
Or at evening in the kitchen, saying
Where are you taking me?
Claiming my index finger in his small hand,
Leaning at forty-five degrees toward
Wherever that may be
And stumbling me outside,
Where we stop, and he makes me look up:
<u>What</u> can you see in the sky?
What can you <u>see</u> in the <u>sky</u>?

II
When I want a line
What I get is a boy
To reel back in from
Grief
Where a dream
Or a cutting tooth
Has drowned him.
What I get is a cry in the night.
What I'm asked to do is to beat out a rhythm
On his body—
As though I were his heart
And he were my soul—
And to sing and make it mean everything
And let it save us both.

III
This is the poem I wrote tonight.

> *I sat in bed reading my friend's quiet poems. You lay asleep beside me, the doors of our bedroom open, the balcony a stage, the drama over, and out on the street the humid night had fallen still. In the figtrees of Arcadia some bats were wakeful yet. In his room at the end of the hall, at the back of this long and slender house, our boy half woke distressed. Something disturbs him some nights. He scratches at his stomach and squirms and cries but only half opens his eyes. And so tonight. Down the honeyed hallway I went to him and lifted him up and carried him creaking downstairs into darkness. I talked gently and wished him back to sleep, but he only cried harder, until I grew exasperated, my peace shot, and I held him firm and rattled him out of it jumping with him and, shaking from him the dream. And somehow that worked, as sometimes it does. Upstairs I heard traffic sighing on Wigram Road as I knelt with him and lay him back upon his mattress, settled into sleep again, and pulled the green blanket over him.*

This is the poem I wrote tonight.

IV
At the end of the street there's a cliff,
And at the foot of the cliff a horse track
Where on Friday nights the trotters race.
And this is the poem the boy spoke,
Looking up at me from his buggy,
As we came home from watching, that first time,
The horses take the final bend of the final race of the night:

Horses   racing   buggies   come-on

The child's the string that played those words,
In whom that race was run.
Now he's the syntax of the broken phrases of his sleep.
And I am the man beside you again,
Reading the poems my friend has written.
I am the very night.

V
I wake on the couch where I have fallen asleep hours before with the boy.
This is long ago, before we were here.
I wake with these phrases ringing:
Out of the bookish hours of the night,
Out of its elegant equations.
And I rise into the first amber moment of morning.
I look down from the kitchen window,
And everything is still and old and early.
The hoop pine is fossilized
And strung with dreams,
Here since long before the land was here
And here again this morning,
And the antique limpid air
Is become a resin in which
Something is entombed.
Back by the bed,
The alarm clock has finished its reading and done its sums,
And it wakes with the answer:
It's time, it tells the morning.
So that the light and my boy can go on sleeping,
So that nothing will ever change,
I slip back and stop the clock.
But already it's too late.
The day stirs.
Time has found it out.

You Know How This Goes,

R IGHT? The morning's the mirror the storm died
    In overnight; the day is distracted
by its own sudden bright solitude. You've dropped
    the little ones at school and the day is

yours and you know this is how contentment
    reads on paper. But you put coffee on
the stove and stand in the sun and feel the
    wind build its case against the way things seem.

And you know there's another life out there you
    were meant to find; there was another face.
You've slipped into someone else's quiet destiny
    and left your run for the beloved too late.

You know how this feels: like she's gone and she's
    never coming back. And you can feel the
afternoon banking in the languor of the morning
    and you can smell the milk boiling over

On the stove. There's no one, it turns out,
    at the wheel. Caught half way between your mind
and your senses, there are moments of sheer
    plunge, and this is one, but, still, you save most

Of the milk and fix a half-decent latte. You carry
    it to the bedroom and sit with it a while,
the light, her pretty bottom tight in her jeans, beside you.
    And when you stand she lies there sleeping on

The white damask spread. When you turn to see
    what turning up again and getting on with it
looks like in the mirror, at your time of life,
    there's no one looking back at you at all.

~

But you know what this feels like. Maybe
    Vincent had it right: *suffering exists*
to remind us that we're not made of wood.
    By midnight you're convinced of it; you've spent

A day back inside the body of your work, and
    the second full moon of the first full
month of the year is smoking her last camel
    in the silence of the Saturday sky.

You look at her and remember the sacred kingfisher
    perched like a floodlight on the real estate
sign for the house by the river at noon. You peer
    back through the black plate of night, cloud

Like mosquitoes on the face of the moon, and you think
    how like his that teal green roshi by the river
had looked in the slant brushstrokes of the lunchtime rain:
    a subject escaped from its frame. *What matters*

Vincent wrote, his heart bright with wheatfields,
    his head dark with crows, *is that one should
learn to want to go on.* A thing the thing with feathers
    never stops at all, but Vincent stopped—we all

Stop, in the end. You hang sometimes, like an infinite
    question, taut between heaven and here.
And the moon, tonight, looking down for her self
    in my window sees only you looking back.

The End of Poetry (As We Know It to Be)

WELL, NO ONE's made it rhyme,
    You know,
Since nineteen-twenty-nine,
    Or so.
But we still got rhythm.
    We got tap,
        we got rap,
            we got postmodernism.

But this ain't no warp in time,
    You know;
We've reached the end of the line,
    You know.
This ain't some bad decision
To unmake
        or to fake.
            This is the final cataclysm.

Amen: A Moment of the World

IF I TOLD YOU rain falls out of a November sky,
    Out of a cosmos of cloud, out of a whole Weather Event,
And the dogs lie at my feet, and I eat breakfast—

Turkish eggs, prepared by the woman who loves me—
    At the round table downstairs, and that eleven o'clock light
Falls into this small room at noon like rain reconstituted

For indoor use, and someone plays an oboe on the radio
    And it sounds like a river pining for the reeds that gather
Like pilgrims on its banks, and at my back stand books

I've carried through four or five lifetimes at least and
    Arranged like the phrases in a poem on these cream
Shelves, where they seem to float like self-satisfied shades,

You might want to dismiss all this—for these are Sadducee
    Days, juridical days—and you might dismiss all this
As just the kind of Pastoral a man like me—privileged by class

And gender and colour and age and half a dozen other entitle-
    Ments and so manifestly unaware of it—might make, mistaking
A moment of his own life for an instance of human experience.

But perhaps it would be different if he told you what the moment
    Is reticent to say—that the eggs are cold because he ran
Late collecting his mother from the cancer clinic,

And the dogs howled for the whole hour in which he was
    Unaccounted for, and the woman he loves was a little put out,
And rightly so, because—like a man—he thought (his mind

Elsewhere at the time) he'd explained that he would gather
    His mother after he'd done the shopping, but then
The clinic, overrun and insufficiently empathetic, like many of us—

He among them, from time to time—had not let him know
    The treatment was running half an hour long, until he called
By and passed the many tests that pandemic protocols set

And had made his way to reception, where they told him
    That half an hour had become an hour, and that they were sorry
They had not called. And he'd not texted this information

In time—concentrated, like a man, on one thing, first
    The shopping, then his mother's cancer, at the expense
Of another, thinking also now and then of his son

Sitting, at that moment, his HSC English paper—to the woman
    Who loves him, so that she'd had to sit and eat by herself this
Breakfast she made for the two of them to share. And now

The tenor sings a sacred song, and on the radio they say the name
    Of a composer who is my friend, and the rain still falls in veils
That reveal only other veils, and some of my book covers curl

In the humid air, and the dogs curl asleep at my feet under
    The round table, its pale wood, and the birds still hide their songs
Inside the tone-deaf weather, except, of course, the Koel,

That town crier, that thief of nests, that coloniser and womaniser,
    That one-hit (two-note) wonder, who, like a naughty child, cares
Only to be heard but never seen. I regret, as ever—and I try

To edit out of what the morning is—the hedge, which crowds
    All freedom out, and tuts like so many tongues who think they know
How to speak and how everyone else should speak and about what,

And to the *photinia robusta* I speak back, saying *your time will come*.
    And so it is that nearly everything, despite appearances, goes on
Being a whole lot other than it had seemed, the morning more

Multiple and even this one life more thoroughly immune
    From easy categorisation than you had thought, and so it always was.
Each self an instance of all such other—manifold and irreducible—

Selves. Each life, all lives. And even I—among many other things,
    This mammal of the masculine persuasion, this son, this father, this lover,
This reader, these notes toward a being, these words—I too am an instance,

It now appears, of a moment of the world. In which the birds
    Are too quiet for my liking and in which all moments are implicated,
All times recalled, not merely these times, *thank god*—times at least

As sure of themselves, as forgetful of what has passed and what
    Endures and half of what counts, as uncertain of the future,
As fearful of death, as all such other times probably always were.

II—*Outside*

The World is Here for its Own Delight

A mind narrows when it has too much to bear.
—Kyo Maclear, "Birds Art Life"

M̲Y MIND today has no account to make
   Of joy. In this it fails the world. And lets
My body down, which wants the day to have
   Her way with it. Later the light and the water
Low in the dam and the flowers that spike on gums
   High on the scarp and the heron that overflies me
As I take the pass south… these fingerprints
   The real world wants to leave on me, imprint,
Anyway, on a speeding mind that knows
   Too little sense to feel them when they land.
But they land. And later—now, for instance—writing
   How little account I have to make, they'll let me
Know I was a fleeting species of
   Delight that had some account to make of me.

Ubirr

This story e can listen careful…
This story e coming through you body…
Tree… yes.
That story e listen.
—Bill Neidjie, "Laying Down"

For Bill Neidjie

THE WORLD is not the place you thought you knew,
    And you, like her, are much more than you seem.
A place on earth is what it makes of you.

Along the scarp a story's listening out
    For you, and who can say who told it first:
The world is not the place you thought you knew.

On your way up, you study the petroglyphs,
    The burrowing bees; you ask them what they mean.
But a place on earth is what it makes of you.

The floodplain tastes like fire; it looks like rain.
    The wind's turning blue—the Wet comes clattering home,
And the world's just not the place you thought you knew.

And who you really are is how you're known
    To everything else—the light, the stone—that's here,
Because a place on earth is what it makes of you.

You turn and find you're not alone—the tree
    Is dancing the afternoon and singing you this:
The world is not the place you thought you knew;
    A place on earth is what it makes of you.

Gaudeamus Igitur

For Barry Lopez

THE WHOLE world composes itself   here. Cedars husband first light
    Along the thin trail I take   to the creek. Log trucks pass along
The road, beside the river,   which makes the quiet fast again.

The slow sun takes its time,   like a mourner, overbrimming hills
    To the east. Morning lights   the distance before it moves in close.
Moss slakes the firs with what   the wrens decant: *while this lasts, rejoice.*

Four Reservoir Tanka

1.
D O YOU THINK the rez,
    This reluctant wetland, cares
That I come among
    Its crestfallen timbers, late
And incapable of love?

2.
I REMEMBER now
    Another day, when two hawks
Spun the shallows still—
    And a squall of firetails, their
Voices an ember attack.

3.
AND ANOTHER: dusk
    A musk across the water's
Mouth. Woods upended
    In the weir, and the dog wild
Among small birds like lament.

4.
THAT DAY one scrubwren
    Flew too slow for cover. I
Stood while, in weeds, she
    Schooled her wing to work again.
My heart, the briar where she flew.

Black Mountain Tanka

T HE MOON is one night
    Old above Black Mountain. June
Winds have littered stars
Across dark hours. Awake with
    Toothache—heartache of the head.

Lichen; or, Saturday Morning Early

ONE DEGREE above freezing at best: a night in June I couldn't wait to end has ended like an era in this scarlet dawn, a reduction of all the light the winter day will yield at length; beneath a wild affray of grey, I take off early into Saturday and walk the grounds of the university in high wind, my dog avid for rabbits, and pulling me like a kite across campus, and I come across a reclining figure, made of wire and fibreglass resin to resemble the local granite; upon her recumbent form only the lichen is real, and she sleeps the sleep of ages among bunch grasses near the Academy of Sciences, dreaming up a plausible way out. Impossible not to stop—unless you're a young spaniel and the lawns are an unexploded ordnance of rabbit droppings, the stands of white gums a seduction of fleeing forms—impossible not to sleep a standing stillness with her half a while. Hard, too, not to reach for a blanket to pull over her, where she rests her head on her prayerful hands. Hard not to want to slip in beside her.

Two Tanka for BL

THE WIND that picks up
    And tosses night's blue-black hair,
Then after midnight
    Helps silence braid it again:
That's my friend, crossing over.

THE CAT comes in from
    The cold and presses her head
Against mine and walks
    My keys: my friend again. Yes.
There's nowhere love is he's not.

Outside: Cantus in memoriam Barry Lopez

For Barry Lopez

1.

After you passed, I carried my life
  Outside. I let it weather the loss
Of you. I carried my work outside:
  Where an order much longer than time
Holds—there, in the fall of Pacific
  Waves on a beach, its crescent almost
Amber with Hawkesbury sandstone tail-
  Ings; in the languid and sweet-talking
Ranks of red gums, salmon in summer

2.

  Rain; on the brow of the promontory,
Tall, like yours, with thought, and far with sight;
  There, among turpentine woods and all
That will not ever be reduced to
  What we want to make it out to be,
Or make it over into: I sought
  Not you, but what you found: what is known,
Almost beyond one's power to know,
  But not beyond one's power to be:

3.
The wisdom enacted in places
    That more or less cohere; cognizance
(To use a word that speaks in your voice),
    Or at least a hint or two, of how
To shape a life of integrity.
    How to lead a life that does some good;
That does some honour to all one's been
    Given. But now I'm trying to say
It, and it flies, like a decade or

4.
    A curlew; it passes like a life.
And still, a week after the cloudburst,
    The rushes on Little Mountain Creek
Lie prostrate, their heads downstream, as if
    In obeisance to a god fled fast.
Walking the dog here is three parts sprint
    And four parts halt—an inadvertent
Interval training, an erratic
    Dance that quickens the ducks from the dead.

5.
I could tell you that by the waters
    Of Mittagong, I lay down and wept,
But it was the waters who did most
    Of the weeping. And half the running.
Some days, though, I slowed and stayed the dog,
    And watched for Rakali, and one day
I saw her at her languorous trawl
    Among the shallows. Her wake was yours.
You taught me more patience than I have

6.
    Time to master; how I go is much
More like the dog. We must each find our
    Own pace, make our own place, take our time.
The day news reached me that you had passed,
    I took your books to the falls and read,
And my love sat beside me on stone.
    The moon rose, one night past full, and three
Black cockatoos flew over us. Hope,
    You wrote, has become a bird's feather,

7.
Glissading from the evening sky, and
    Ever since, walking, I keep finding
Feathers. As if the sky had made off
    In haste, chased perhaps by this rude dog.
I carry them inside and press them
    Between the leaves of your book *Outside*,
Where I found two feathers already—
    This white one, small as a coin, this blue
Jay's. And now this wood duck's taupe plume and

8.
This—black above, white under—magpie—
    And this, gun grey with a scarlet chevron
At its tip. You'd ask where I'd found them;
    You'd ask about each bird. All I know
Is: if beauty's the thing with feathers,
    She may be losing air. It seems right
To enter every place with sadness,
    Seeking mercy there, being glad for
Every bird that flies and feather that

9.
Falls. For wisdom is both light and grave.
    And every pretty place has cost ten
Lives at least, and all that seems a gift
    Was stolen once and must be given
Back. You practised on us all the care
    You could have used when you were young. Each
Word forgave what nothing can forgive.
    Let me walk your work outside and fledge
From feathers a canticle of birds.

We Are Not Finished at the Skin—
A Cradle Mountain Suite

1. COMING IN

THE WORLD is made of rock, I think,
As we take a cold hard bend; the world
Is made of music. Even the rock
Is made of music.
                But the morning
Is made of rain, a looser kind
Of arrangement, and the rain falls
On bus windows, which are steaming fast
And stealing the landscape from me,
And the rain returns the basalt cutbanks
To the fluid state the rock once was,
Back when the music was hot
And the world itself was young.

2. THE RIVER

For a week, I've sat in this hut in the rain,
Alone in a forest of pines. I know
I'm blessed to be here alone with my work
And the weather, and words have come like rain,
As often and as long. But now I'm running low,
And so this afternoon I walk along Dove River,
The loveliest quarter of the valley.
Rain comes and goes and goes and comes
Among the black pencil pines,
And the river carries the lake away,
The colour of cold billy tea.
It roils and mewls, engorged with storms,
And I hear stones roll on the river's bed
Like longing in my stomach.

3. Sin

I am tired of gentleness and geologic
Time, of discipline and moss and rain; I want
To sin. A small offence would do—
To be drunk and wanton with the girl
I love, rude together, carelessly
Untying each other's rhythmic knot.
But I'd almost settle for a smoke.

3. GEOLOGIC TIME

A body of water

Strata go straight up here
And rain comes straight down.
At the lake's edge two cypress pines
Stand petrified,
Waiting for the weather to clear
Before they plunge; a hundred years more
And their chance may come.
Meantime they lean like arthritic ghosts
Their thinning branchlets livid green
Into another cold summer gale.
The water in the blunt grey basin
Is the black of time before time
And the aubergine of a coming storm.

Storm & bird

There's a currawong at the lookout as black
And wet—in our coats, I mean, in this rain—
As I am. He tries, but looking solicitous
In weather like this is a hard trick
To pull off. He throws me a fierce, slant
Vermilion glare, which sums me up fast
As good for nothing but words, and
He shrugs off the rain and takes cover.

Landscape photography
I turn and take the ten thousand steps
Up the stone mountain and the rain swarms
Down. Go back. Don't go back. Go back.
I've rarely sworn at weather before
But this is getting personal. When
I make the top, still in the ice cold
Rain and the mobbing wind, I find
I've shot my last frame down below.
So, here's what Cradle Mountain looks like
Beside me: a worn and rusted axe-head,
Blade up; and here are four lakes
Arrayed to receive the antique runoff
Down among button-grass sloughs and glacial
Mounds and wombats and dour cypress woods—
Chaste, impecunious brotherhoods of brown.
And here's all this concatenated rock,
Paused in its emphatic articulation
Of the slow history of the earth. Here is one
Poised moment evading capture.

5. HUMAN TIME

On the cold roof grey rain falls;
Later it will turn to snow.
The heater churns on and on
And I've put myself to bed
In a narrow bunk in a
Night as dark as a mineshaft.
Desire wells where words lay
In seams before I mined them.
Years ago when I first saw
You I was empty, too, and you
Fell on me like rain and welled
Into the only love poem
I can write anymore. And
Tonight I waited as though
You might come again, as though
I were not waiting at all;
I found paths to walk and a
Meal to make and slowly eat
And dishes to wash and poems
To read and darkness to watch
Come down and sometimes a night
Lasts as long as a mountain.

8. MUSE

And the next night she drives up
And looks in my window and
Sees me looking over my
Laptop at whoever she
May be, and she walks to my
Door and says she's down at Kate
House by the river. Photo-
Graphs are what she does and what
She's doing here—photographs
And soup—and am I working
Tomorrow night? What do you think?

7. KINDS OF LOVE

You don't take love; you make it,
Like a photograph, she says.
And if you look through the lens
Long enough at any place

Or anyone what you see
Is infinity. And she
Has a body like you
Never saw, and you will be

Undone, in time, like the mountain.
There are many kinds of love,
And all day long, with the rain,
She makes the kind you make by

Letting fall everything that
Isn't really you at all
And making of yourself a
Picture the landscape can take.

And all night long by gaslight
The mountain decorates her
In red and makes her his own.
And the mountain tells her: We

Are not finished at the skin.
But something is, for it is
In our bodies that we know
Each other as something

Altogether other than
We are alone. Where we touch
You'll find a world without end.
And down by the lake the moon

Comes out and frames a woman
Standing at the edge looking
Up at the mountain. Are you
Ready? she asks; are you sure?

And the water turns white and
The mountain goes black and the
Sky above is silver and
Swimming with cloud. Her shadow

Is cast into the lake. Cloud
Shutters the moon; the image
Is made, the woman is gone,
And the night is the night again.

8. ERRATICS

There are kettle holes in the floor
Of heaven; there's even a twisted
Lake. There are creeping
Pines and strawberry pines
And devil scat and dwarf pines
And petrified wood and schist.
And just over there, pencil
Pines are drawing the edge of
The water. There are bones, too.
Some belonged to young souls lost
Long ago in the weather,
And some of them are trees,
Trying to become angels.
The kind that haven't fallen
Yet. Down below, high clouds swim
The lake, making believe it's
Summer. And up by the tarn,
Where the mountain walks back
Into view along the track,
Just past the spot where Roy and
John stopped and named for me most
Of the flowers and plants of
The woodlands of Tasmania—
Fagus and white epacris
And pink boronia down
Among the great king billies—
She lay down in the blue
Afternoon and let the night
Love her and this morning's what
They made. To return to earth,
To rise again, hold the chain-

Rope tight and step a thousand
Metres down into the lake
Where night lies very still.

9. GOING OUT
The bus cuts north, taking me
Home. Something that will never
End has come to an end and
I pass at speed two tractors
Rusted to a standstill in
A slow red potato field.

Five Soft Nets: A Coledale Sonnet Cycle

1.

A<small>T THE BACK</small> of the beach,
We hunt among the painted
Stones for Coledale. With our toes among pools
And losing our feet, we try to divine, as if one could,
A place. Come always into country humbly, knowing it has meant the world—
And means it still—to someone. Across this tessellated shelf
Two continents at least of syllables and time, of bloodshed
And dance steps, have stranded and are
Reassembled daily, by violence and grace,
Into this high estate, this sooty-oyster-captured place, along
This whalebone shore. I know too little
To say too much, so I speak
Only to bribe the kids to open
Their eyes to rarer birds than gulls,

2.
To petition the shallows
To sing. The first time I came
The summer was high; the second, the sky was low—
As if the heavens the holiness came down from
Were keen to take a little of it back. Beginning with the scarp, where
Clouds, those turps-soaked *rags of time*, have reclaimed
Ten millennia and whited out the turpentine and coachwood
Halfway down to Cokeworks Road.
Merrigong crowds the beaches here
All year; its feet are made of shale and coal and potter's clay
And spelling mistakes, and in among the cliffs
Behind the shore, where we fossick
The shelf like shorebirds, my children find
A niche and in that small crypt

3.
The turquoise of a yabby's
Tail, some honeysuckle,
An orange claw. Relics. Spare parts. And our bird
Count is up—swallows tossing out
Rude welcomes on the wing; wagtails, acrobats of the wrackline,
Singing glad farewells among the kelp; bulbuls;
A tern or two; a curlew; and a whitefaced heron headed south.
Coledale, where we look for her
In the ebb of afternoon, looks
Like a festival of fallen kites, a tidal tailings dam
The goddess steps over in her Blundstones
At pains to be a coastal
Range again by dusk. The place
We find is a jumble sale

4.
Of mantle-piece gods and random
Aircraft parts and forty-
Seven colourful false-starts, and in the green rockpools
Zebra-striped snails and blue periwinkles
Describe curvilinear songlines—stories whose plots, like ours, are lost
On us; whose lyrics are how these strata learned
To bend. The place that finds our feet
Is a linocut of flyways and tide-
Lines, of starfish and beaches
And breaches and beginnings again. My mother,
It happens, was born in these measures, not far north,
In the settlements they spawned,
The forgetting they begot.
Coal spells many things,

5.
And only some of them well.
Coal parsed this place, which surpassed
Again, in time, the coal they (mis)named it for. A dale, it seems,
Knows much more than its seams. And here, behind
The beach I find a stone, a motherlode, a motherboard, in whose form
And tone the circuitry of this aubergine, this green
And ochre, this stolid and tender, this linear
And round-cornered world
Is spoken—the whole *contracted*
Thus. It's a heavy kite, a skew-weft slate on which
Is spelled out this: A place is a mind
You may come to share;
A heart laid open by birdsong
And tides; a body made supple
By love.

The Godwit Shores

For Jodie Williams

I DON'T MIND the rain at all,
                       you said. A small articulation of how it is
    You've learned to live so well. There's nothing much
You don't know how to weather or divine,
    In time, a way to practise care upon.
                            Like these birds, who fly the bright
And quiet news of you on seasonal loops around the earth,

A miracle lost on all but the few who look
                    but also see among three generations
    Lost to all that matters (except themselves), you walk a light-footed
Electricity of hope across the tidal flats, you fathom
    A feast from unpropitious shores,
                         and you fly, when you're ready, a flight
    Of immaculate affection for where you find yourself and where

You'll likely find yourself next—some farther place,
                       some sedgeland, some selvedge, some steppe.
    And this year, for your birthday, the heavens chose to pour
Where last time they'd shone, and you found no less
    Joy in that. Happiness is what happens
                    and how you practise that with love: this
Is what your life tells, its art the same art as these shores.

Estuary

I COME walking on the broken basalt
               of the point that keeps the swell—wild this morning after nights
   Under southerly winds—from the tidal flats, and overnight the sea,
A panic of waters, has disgorged
   A shark—a wobbegong—among the kelp and coral,
                     and some among the crows, the curlews and the oystercatchers—
Pied and sooty—have taken out his eyes.

The dog, sniffing everywhere, encounters the carpet shark
                        and starts: his astonished stiff-limbed sideways jump
   A vaudeville routine. An animal knows an animal, even in death,
From a plant; prey discerns predator, no matter
   How cold. The scent of danger, like the sense of occasion,
                             never wants to disappear. The shelf curves
Like a well-used whetstone, and the swell comes at it soft and ineluctable,

Like it means, at last, to get this right. My mind is such
                  a stone, worn by so much love, the weight of it taking the edge off
   All that's unthinkable now. And standing here among the birds,
Flighty among their fortune, I feel through my feet
   All the energy pent and voluptuously spent
                        in each wet assay, and I turn from the sea
And walk south. Love is so like water, the tide in things, the calm

And the affray. And in behind the haptic edge, we walk
                              a shore of stone, the dog at his devotional and I,
    Less devoutly, at mine, and the shore is a seaweed
Collector's handbook, its pages frayed and flung, its reeds unread, its kelp unkempt,
    Its bladderwrack redacted, its tangleweeds unspooled
                          like syntax unstrung, like bells unrung:
A magpie lark alights on the open mouth of a fisherman's bag,

And doesn't fly her ziplock roost when we walk past.
       The fisher—extreme acupuncturist, Hokusai with a rod—throws,
    Meanwhile, his line into the passing wake of the tallest wave, and retreats
In spume, like a wader, to the higher ground we stalk. The morning is still
    Too soon to wrest my mind from its salvage and register
                            much of any of this, so I turn again
And after coffee find a way, with a pen, to live where I went

For all that it was worth. The tidal flat where our cabin rests
                        is a canvas stretched for water to prime and wind
    To daub and crabs to hole and godwits to festoon.
The shallows, with their pelicans and tangle-haired spaniels, their tertiary blues
    And corduroy browns, their restless ease, are a watercolourist's impression,
                        a tone poem for strings and a solitary oboe,
Of every childhood summer once and incipient old age. I think I may

Get to my father's age, his ninety years, and still
                              not trust in my heart what the estuary knows in its waters.
    We came in late last night, the spaniel, my love and I,
And this morning, when the tides fall from the shoulders of the sands,
      Among the debris of the deeper sea the rip had dragged in,
                        I see that the godwits are back—three birds
Divining the flats, fuelling for flight, improving the light,
           pulling the distance taut, their reddening bills wise
                   to what sleeps just beneath the surface of this sometimes
                              floating world.

Dolphin Point

For Jodie Williams

P ERHAPS, LOVE, we are like the two eagles, who surf
    The break-neck breeze above the basalt
Shore at dusk, quartering the moon
        between us, the intemperate tide at bay

    Beneath us. Perhaps, love, like the birds, we hang here easy in the eye
Of a southerly gale, held like a breath above the affray,
              two years as fast as a fortnight behind us,
    The day already a decade deep.
              (And miles to go... and miles.)

South Coast Sedoka

For Jodie Williams

WHY DO two godwits
   Choose these tidal flats, this day,
Where we walk two years of love?

TWO days among trees
   In a small house like a tent,
Lashed to earth with whipbird riffs.

WHEN our dog draws close
   Across the tidal flats, four
Godwits launch. And circle back.

WHEN FIRE has burned down
   Half the life you knew, how fine
To find this creek, these sheoaks.

THE BANKS so low, the green creek
   So high, and a steady rain:
To walk here's to swim.

Among the Lighted Woods with Dante; or, Sheoaks at Sanctuary Point

For J; for D

Sheoaks throw shadows as if they were glass.
           Along the shore they winnow the wind; from the chaff
  Of the silence they harvest a past. And in the shallows,
              which redouble the winter light
Into a violet incandescence, a single heron makes her small mirrored
  Deliberations; she strikes and shakes her head and swallows and stakes
Out another antiphonal claim. Her gestures refined—
            her predation a Sanskrit of limpid attention.
  Among the trees, we pass like a murmur, shepherding the pup,

Who's a clumsy choreography in love
           with all the newness in the world: saltmarsh, mangrove
  Roots, the brackish bitterness he licks from the lips of the water's edge,
Shags on the point of the pier. The bark
           of a bigger dog chastens the young one to our side. Till he finds,
  A moment later, another scent to sound.
           Among the keening of the trees, one is the distance
Of low hills, and the place is a mind one shares. We stand a moment,
  Still, within the inner life of time; we walk home along a threshing floor,
           blue with afternoons fallen from trees like a dissident music.
                 Like an indigent shade.

Whitefaced Heron Above the Green Creek

       T HE WIND
    Is boisterous, and the light
        A reduction of saffron and summer
  Rain. December 6, when, every year,
Every year comes unstuck. If purple were a sound,
    This would be it: the grinding of gears as the heron, as if this were
Her first attempt, the afternoon her grandfather's car,
    Double-declutches
        Down inside the Dresden light and—unfolding
    Her legs like an elaborate excuse—
Finds the upper reaches of a turpentine,
        Which stands the banks
    Of this green stream, and becomes its grey
      And panelbeaten canopy.

Ghazal of the Weather Upon the Lake

For Peter Lustig

AT DAWN the stillness of the lake is all that's broken in one's heart;
    By noon, the heart's grown still, the weather wild, and the mild waters fraught.

Didn't the real world always run like this? And through it all—the birds:
    As if they flew the paradox of things; as if their bright wings taught

What all our words are slow to learn—the promise in the price. The prize
    That sometimes earns what all the years have cost. The egret stands the shore

In drought; she stands it in the storm. The black swan trawls the afternoon
    As if it were the dawn. The game of life's a contradictory sport,

A holy kind of comedy, in which the way to heaven's hell—
    And sometimes back—and all you want is peace, and all you get is riot.

The morning's a circus of clouds—and just as it ends, first rain falls.
    All the weather knows is change. Love holds true, but half of love is doubt.

How hard it is to inhabit what hurts, till it yields, till harm heals;
    To home like the godwit through gales, to catch what can never be caught:

The breath of the wind on the water; the shadow that throws the light;
    The myth inside the minute; the freedom that schools an exile heart

To keep compassion's beat. Nothing in nature knows how to miswant—
    Flight wants the feather, the feather the bird: the beginning the word,

It's been said. The dawn breeze is the vespers the sheoak wants to hymn.
    If the lake wants its fill, it must tide out the storm the winter's wrought.

All afternoon, egrets and cormorants traffic a contraband
    Calm toward the leeward shore. Evening feels like morning's last resort.

And tomorrow rages all night, the winds the dogs of war, the rain
    As thick as *The Lives of the Saints*, a peace that must be sagely fought

At dawn. The wilderness of the lake is all that's tempered in your heart.
    And into the rain the egret flies the alphabet of your art.

Flood Tide

As I sat in the last ebb of day,
                turning over last thoughts
  At the small table beside the turpentines, first one
And then the other of a nesting pair of herons
                              flew low from the lake shore,

Where they had been feeding
                the long day together in the flood tide,
  And the blue grace notes of their flight toward
The fallen sun redeemed, it seemed, the hard
                        industrial clangour of the voices they followed home.

Flat Rock, September

For Lucy & Henry

IN THE POTHOLES, which know no floor my feet
    Can find, the moments pool, while years disappear

Downstream, and time strains eras from the hanging
    Swamps; it drums up aeons where they've slumped

In siltstone strata—and slips them like silk over skin
    Where these two streams run a shallow skein over stone.

Eternity's made of moments that don't know how
    To pass, and one of them's not passing here this late

September afternoon in the upper reaches
    Of a long contagious year of the warming world.

Behind the scarp that wraps us round, the day
    Is shutting down. Light swells above the waters

Before it falls behind the cliffs, and dusk
    Is a vivid shrapnel raining down the amber

Air—a million flying things that rise
    From figs and watergums to take the season's

Bait. These resurrected larvae, late
        To lunch, launch, in the dying of the day,

A reenactment of flight's first spawning.
    Our moment in the stolen stream, our little

Stay of time's quick flow, is overflown
        By a swarming metamorphosis, rank

On rank of life's insistence on itself,
    Death's re-creation of the real. The stream was

My daughter's idea, and we raced the day along
        The gravel track to arrive before it closed—

The road washed out on half the bends, and on
    A hanging limb a whipbird, white headphones on,

One half of the sweetest antiphon that silence
        Knows, a bird that makes a hideout of

Her song—and now my daughter swims the twilight
    Waters, thick with Icarus bits, and she's trying

Not to breathe too many of the fallen
        In. The dying's a calm and holy thing,

A meteor shower drowned and become a stranding
    Of light, an ephemeral benediction upon

A stream—a litany of silences still strung
        In my daughter's hair when she calls me in

To fathom, if I can, the deeps. Time plays
    No favourites. Here or anywhere. Time passes

No judgment: she knows nothing of endings;
    Nor ever begins again. And death's a space that's left

For life to fill. A slack that living stretches
    Taut again. Later, I hear what my body knew—

Its reluctance to enter in: these are women's
    Waters, this blithe cemetery, this nursery

Of flight, this river's bed, whose floor my falling
    Refused to find. We steal the places from them-

Selves; we steal the river from the women
    It blessed; the children it birthed; the dead.

At least let there be honour among us
    Thieves. It is a second baptism, then, I sink,

A grateful fear I plumb, a blasphemy
    I swallow swilling a prayer of gratitude

For a chance I had no right to hope would come—
    To swim an evening river with my kids, to drop

As deep as I dare, still to find no end
    To how far back the present moment

Runs. So much has had to end to let
    This be. So let this be—this reprieve, this reprise—

The honour we bear, the penance we pay, the past.
    Let us walk together, quick with coming cold, across

Flat rock, glad for lives that float a while yet.

Inland

For Elizabeth Coleman

I

WEST of the divide smells like
    Sadness and eternity,
Smells like ancient history
    And forgiveness. Smells like red
Gravel and white spinifex.

II

    I take the plane's rear stairs out
Into the aftermath of
    Rain down onto slick tarmac.
Canberra. Brindabellas.
    A good sheep station ruined.
Not far west, but far enough.

III

    West of the divide, the land
Smells like itself, not the sea.
    It smells like country, old, old
Rain, like cattle and granite.
    Inland the air has the tone
Of sheoak and cockatoo,
    Dry creek and geology—
A dry peneplain of doubt.

IV
    Wherever you are, the smell
Of rain coming or just gone
    Is the smell of the same rain
Locally inflected. Here
    It's limestone and politics,
Paddocks and poplars and grief.

V
    West of the divide smells of
Lichen and salt and dryness
    Itself, bore water and wheat
Silos, crows' cries and distance.
    A continent of long time.

VI
West of the divide smells like
    Where you'd want to come from if
You knew who you really were.

The Hill Again

For my children

AFTER YEARS, I walked the hill again today.
Summer has taxed the country hard, and the days
Have burned too long.
        The light among the trees
Was low in mood, muted and subdued —
The penumbra of fires north and south.

I passed the wombats, cast in bronze, where children,
Mine, and I among them, used to play.
Alone, I crossed the bridge that spans the creek
That never runs,
        and I held out my hand to steady
My girl who used to walk its railing like

A beam: she never used my hand, but the balance
She kept, from end to end, depended on
My being there.
        And how does she do it now?
Further along, the undergrowth crackled with snakes,
Sated with sun and glad enough to clear

My way. The half-made track was a holiday
Crowd of rabbits, laying out their blankets
For a picnic under stars,
                        and the way they scattered
Inside the bracken as I came, you could tell
They thought they'd seen the back of me.
                                    At the top,

Where I stopped and sat on a bench and keyed some notes
From this old familiar field, a king parrot
Showered in the shade of barrel gums
And looked about ready to abdicate and let
The republic come.
                 A place is a space, I read

Today, to which a meaning is ascribed.
I came to lay myself again among
The meaning this one makes—
                          this timbered place
A story that had stopped reciting me
And those I loved.
                   I went to make a place

Again for them, to walk a story once
Upon a time again and never end.
To divine a place in which the past will never
Cease to tell
          and futures breathe like memories
Of trees. I took the broken steps and pressed

On to the trail's end.
                And there the distance
Drew itself together into the kind
Of thing I had in mind—
                        the down still that upland
We used to dream we'd climb, the sky an invisible
City where all undoing comes undone.

Hammock Hill Haiku

The mist has burned off
And a thousand spiders sleep
Late in their daybeds.

Up

THE THIRD time I pass him on the stair,
                    Dave, the cleaner, puts it this way:
Living four flights up might make you
Think twice before you left
                    your shopping in the car.

But you only have to look
                    at me to know that's not (always)
Going to be true, and, sure enough, after a month
I'm as fit as a trout
              in a midsummer night's stream.

Each trip too good to take
                  only once, the way up and the way
Back, and so on, and on, a joke bespoke in your voice,
My love, a sixty-two step program
                    in levity and gravity.

And I like it up here
                  among the morning prayers of friar-
Birds, among the blackfaced cuckoo-shrikes
And the wail of departing vessels,
                    making away with the night in the night.

I like it up here, as high
                    as you can get above
The belly-flopped port and still have your feet
On the ground, where the meta
                    meets the physical;

Where the body of the world
                    thinks its thoughts
In several languages and hope blows in
On storm fronts from the south.

Wait

I WAIT for poetry as if it weren't waiting at all;
As if waiting were a river at the end of summer,
    A dream with its boots on, a walk among
The dead; I wait as if waiting were a matter
    Of sitting here by the shore over coffee
With the dog (who waits, as if born waiting,
    Over water in a bowl); I wait as if waiting were
The grace that lets me take as long as the waiting
    Wants to take, untroubled by militias, malarias,
Creditors, taxes, tides. I wait for poetry as if waiting
    Were the fish and I the line. As if poetry were love
And had all day. I wait as if I hadn't waited fifty-
    Three years already; and when at last she comes,
I see that she's been sitting here beside me all along.

The Hill

        1.

        M<small>Y PLACE</small> is a belfry,
And I am its bell. I am rung—some days
        I am carilloned—by light. I am improvised
By unrehearsed skies.
        The days are my riffs, no pitch, no key,
No melody. A wild and necessary music
        That doesn't know how to stop.
        Hours utter me, minutes
Stutter me. Silence cries me, and I am
        The shadows that other days spill
Like birdsong at the feet
        Of this fine day
        And the next.

    2.
    Here, I am
Every life I might have lived
    And maybe did, rendered specifically
As if it mattered
    To be said as one is. I am a shoreline
Of stories four storeys high, a miscellany of breezes. I am
    The wolves in night's pages, the starlings
At dawn. I am a murmuration of pigeons.
    An unbecoming storm.
        A view without a room.
I am a blindman's mirror.
        History's flapping page.

The Halflife of Coal

1. Above

THERE IS NO blue without yellow, and there's no green without blood
Red. The wall that leads from the kitchen looks like Wittenoom

In the dry. Spinifex rings of mortar collapse exquisitely into
The afterlife among the pieces they used to hold apart. Green

Paint blackens to blue and falls like spent leaves from scarps
After fire. How many women have run their hands like rivers

Along these pitted bricks incarnadine, on their way to
The well out the back? There is no death without life,

And the last life lived here stopped in 1963. Charles
Milligan Little is killed and the house stands unused: the panel

Reads like a bad translation of a doleful incantation from
The Egyptian Book of the Dead and the house feels as empty

As a tomb. Charles Milligan Little doesn't live here anymore.
The pieces of who he was here have been scattered

Like the body of Osiris, carried in coal tankers this time,
To the ends of the late industrial Earth. In the kitchen

There's a tap without a basin, and no one stopped the papers
Till late September '65. All over the walls nature has been

Remembering herself in dendritic pictographs since the day
The house began forgetting what it had meant. *Now's the time*

To start building the physique you want for summer, I read
One month in 1964. (Even then, it was way too late for that.)

Have You Seen This Baby? asks *The Daily Telegraph* another day,
And *Two Gun Theory in Murder*. There is no life without death.

Down the hall time has passed violently at least once—
The earthquake of '89 or subsidence has opened a seam

In the plaster wide enough to mine. There isn't an order
Of emptiness not showcased in these rooms. Some is papered

In blue and grey and some is Empire pink, and here the ceiling slumps
Between its battens, out of its mind with missing the child, perhaps,

Who slept here once. Poetry, they say, recalls the other language,
Close cousin of silence, that's lost inside the gossip and the news,

But no one's saying much of anything in here. All one has is surface
And bright autistic spaces strung with thick asbestos webs. Still,

The past is in here somewhere: for there's no present without a past,
And here we are. To forget the past, it is said, is to plant cut flowers

In your garden, and plainly there's no future in that. Nor is there any
Future in what this house oversaw for sixty years, an industrious addiction

That's cost us all the earth. You can feel it coming in the savage heat
Of this early summer morning. From up here you can almost make it

Out along the grey horizon, one huge vessel after the other, disgorging
Its bilge, emptying itself to receive the black and broken body of the god.

2. *Between*

BY AFTERNOON, the old-world order has gone under.
The wind is rising and the sea is rising
And the map of the old world
Is in way above its head.

Sand has buried the continents we used to know.
In particular it's outwitted that pretty Edwardian idea,
Which you could paint any colour anywhere
As long as it was pink and tell

In any tongue as long as it was this one.
The map of the world is full of water today—
Of language and silvergulls and promise and girls
Who don't care what you think their bikinis

Are trying to say to you. There's an onshore breeze
And a chop on the afternoon water and a green rind
On the breakwater that used to keep the pink empire afloat,
And pretty soon, you can tell, the sun's going to set on all of it.

3. *Below*

THERE IS NO light without darkness. And it's dark as hell
Down here. They've drained the pool where the soldiers

Used to dally (a little too wantonly it seems) and dive
And they've bricked it over and plunged it into nothing-

Ness—the kind of nothing that might teach you something,
If only you could find your way down. No one to guide you,

You follow in your own footsteps to the underworld
Beneath the commercial light of day. Every night Osiris, re-

Membered and loved again to death, slips down here
From Hunter Street to make another downpayment

On tomorrow and buy more stars for heaven from among
The ungrateful dead below. You're just here to window shop,

But that's what they all say. It's what Dante said, too,
When he was caught out light years later in the middle

Of the dark shopping mall of his days. You've left your book
Of posthumous charm back on your hotel bed. You've for-

Gotten your map of the baths of the dead, so you're just going
To have to wing it. You can't see to save yourself, in any case.

But could those be the shades of soldiers, smoking
By the seventh gate in striped turn-of-the century togs?

And surely that's the son of the foreman of the Mine
Of Imperishable Stars, playing cards with his Sunday

School teacher. Is it rude to ask "How are you?" of men
Who no longer are? And don't look now, but isn't that

Osiris, swimming slow world-weary laps in green re-
Surrected speedos? Or maybe it's Charles Milligan Little

Killing time in the shallow end of the Pool of the Blue
Hippopotamus till someone comes to remember him

Again. But one shouldn't make light of the dark like this.
In truth, there's nothing here but a disembodied coal-seam

Of regret. This is what abandonment might look like
If you could only make it out—the silt of the arcade's

Substrate settling like the prayers of children in the deep
End of the century before last. Darkness pooled so densely

Could teach daylight what it's for. And so you turn and take
The stairs back up into all that's grown too bright for us above.

Revelation Days

For Ali and Thomas

THE DAYS have turned Biblical, warnings
    Come to pass. Warmings come home. Home
Become prodigal. Prophesied dooms become
    The rooms in which we still refuse to wake.
Jung always said that uncomfortable truths
    We could not acknowledge in our natures
Would grow monstrous in the dark of our
    Inattention, until they took over the joint
We thought we ran.
                        And so one day
    It's fires burning all the green in every
Southeast forest brown and downing every
    Song; and the next day it's the drought
Come to town on the north wind, a red scrim
    Varnished over everything at dawn;
And on the next day, it's hail hard as artillery
    Fire and cold cluster bombs on the capital;
And for many days then, it's smoke where sun–
    Light used to play, smoke become the nation's
Largest export, after coal and overpriced
    Education; until it's fire again, for these are
Days you cannot douse, and then it's Darling
    Showers, and then it's thunderstorms at
Breakfast, when you could've done with them

    At dusk, when the day refused to cool,
Or the seabreeze, where it always washes in,
    To come; and just for a moment in a morning
Rain the miners make a contrapuntal noise
    About, you could almost begin again
To imagine that we and all the living
    Things the temperate earth had hosted for
So long had not become the weather's orphans,
    The days a climatic concentration camp,
The suburbs the leading edge of the sort
    Of catastrophe you conjure by neglect.
And on the windchime's tip one drip hangs
    Tough against all that wants to change,
And the rain falls on and on. And stops.
    And comes again.

Above the Snowies on the Day of First Snow

For Jodie Williams

THE PILOT promised it and there it lay, a crust of cloud on one reach of ridge—one snow storm, a dry run for winter, instantiated there, and all these burnished forests like ancestral days around, ways that have outlasted so far all our little virtues and our larger sins, and outlived all the fire storms our economic forecasting will yield. These ranges run a slim and angular swagger just like the one my child walks, a cheeky introversion, a quiet iconoclasm, refusing very calmly to conform. Above the gorges—here, now, above the Eildon Weir—valley cloud flocks; it flies, motionless, a holding pattern; it fashions a stasis untroubled by all that agitates our everydays; it makes above the hollows a soft and archetypal replica of the harder form that falls from clouds and holds the ridgetops down. The same kind of second self we enter into sometimes and flesh out, as a dream fleshes sleep, gone again at morning, but known in one's body a long time after, as if a wider mind than one's own had flared and woken you to every other self you also are.

And again, as the plane loses altitude, a frosting on the forests looks at first like winter's wash, but these are the companies of souls, the mountain ash, standing on yet, ancestors not properly interceded for, that burned in fires more savage than any they had learned to refute, as we, who have not prayed a hard enough thanks for the trees and the snow and the way the blue world has gone, will not be ready, either, for the shape of all that comes.

The Jetty

For Donna Ward

I WALKED a mile out to sea
    all the way to the end
of the long memory of the jetty—
    a mile from shore on cantillated
concrete—to harvest the violet

Weather. There's a whole order of secondhand
    trees cloistered beneath these
slabs beneath my feet; they spent a forest
    to ship a forest
to the backstreets of the world. To anchor

A town to its unholy destiny. But it turns out
    this folly has manifest worlds
in the tepid and secular water that it shades.
    There are numb rays and green
sea-hares and twenty styles of leatherjacket.

There are red mosaic starfish and black-banded
    sea-perch. There are vermillion
nudibranchs and chameleon squid
    and well-tempered seadragons
playing with fire in the seagrass meadows

Of Geographe Bay. There's a gloomy
        octopus with a spanner in one hand
and if we don't take it off him
        he'll have the whole thing down
by Christmas. So it turns out

This is not our jetty at all. This is not
        our floating earth and that's not
our grave and shallow sea below. Turns out
        the jetty is their heaven, and we,
their omnivorous pelagic gods, their everyday

Industrial strength constellations:
        Orion over there in board-shorts
dealing death with a ten-pound line
        and the four hundred thousand
denim-clad Pleiades from the suburbs.

I wonder if the dusky morwongs know
        this is still the longest
ephemeral structure in the southern
        hemisphere. I wonder
if the schools of fashion-conscious yellow-

Fins care that the old jetty is slumping
        into retirement in a nursing home
on the coast. The past speaks
        a splintered diction only the timber
now recalls, and the sea trafficks a brilliant

Contraband on the currency
       of tides. And if you stood here
long enough in the fickle winter rain,
       you might come to know yourself
the way the jetty knows

The bay and the cormorant
       knows the habits of the crab.
You might find eternity
       in a concrete slab and romance
in an ephemeral pool of blood.

The Bay

THE MORNING is a hand-
                tinted photograph torn from Life
  Magazine late one afternoon in 1956. In which paradise
Decomposes sweetly beneath the mission brown boards of a hut,
    And a man sits, remembering too thickly and breathing too thin,
And the bay, in the shining robes of a Siddha, finds shore
                                and finds it again. The sea at its karma
    Along the coral beach is the fierce blue mind
                      of the kingfisher, making plans
                                      on the powerlines even now.

The sky here is a mile
                too big for the bay's boots. Savusavu—
  This flooded arena in which nothing much, on the surface of things, ever happens,
To the enormous delight of the cava-mellowed mob of semi-superannuated
    Mountains in their green flak jackets
                            and their greener fatigues—Savusavu
Is morality play in countless acts of cloud
    And itinerant weather. It's where the water cycle of the whole wide world comes to dress

Rehearse. At evening, the coconut palms
                        crane their crooked necks to watch
  The sunset turn water into wine. They're still there,
Leaning at erratic, companionable angles, when,
                                  backlit by the bawdy moon,
  The clouds compose a frantic tectonic map of the world, and then map it all over again.
In the darkness, the susurrus of the bay resumes, and the blue boat drones sheepishly home
    From oyster grounds,
               and fruit bats and geckos pick up roughly
                                where the weavers and mynahs left off

In the dusk, and on the deck, the man paces.
                              He's spent the day in books and birdsong,
  And he's come away with nothing to show for it. The amber-eyed kitten,
A stray and infantile muse who's found him here,
                          too late to do either of them any good,
  Bats wildly at mosquitoes drawn to the violet neon light, downs a moth
And swallows it alive. The green bus passes
               on the road from the resort
                   like an infantry battalion, flags of conversation
  Streaming from its windows. Given time, he thinks, everything,
              even the saddest thing, will be recounted in the bright vernacular of love.

Jimbaran Bay, Late October: An Accidental Love Song

Along the shore the women
    Come and go, speaking of Pialago,
Touching the water as if it were skin
    And they were silk. At the next

Table the Sri Lankan toddler cries
    Again. She's almost cleared the beach.
With lychee martinis and cigarette
    Kisses, the Egyptian lovers patch up

The quarrel they walked in with. Kadek
    From Nyoman's Warung refreshes
The offerings to the officious deities
    Of the beachfront. A palm leaf tray

Of petals and rice and burning incense.
    The whole of heaven is appeased;
The whole afternoon is pleased. There are
    No flies. There are no birds. No breeze.

Only the toddler's cries, and the woman
    In the red one-piece making love
To the tune in her head, dancing alone
    On the tip of the Indian Ocean's tongue.

At My Brother's House

For John Sullivan

THIS IS what the tropics are for:
     I sit late at the dining table alone,
           inside and outside
 At once. The night eases by. Frogs crow and barrack.
One makes a fat man's flashdance across the terrazzo.
       Two fans turn in compound low

  Above. And behind me, water falls soft and perpetual
        into the lap pool, streaming
           from the fat penis of some impious minor deity.
In the pavilion, a one-armed Vishnu sleeps the good sleep
  In chiaroscuro. If enlightenment can't find you here,
        you've been kissing the wrong angels.

Tropicbird

We sat together on the stone. The forest below us
Steamed after rain, and I knew this was your idea
Of paradise. A place like this, you said to me,

> *You either leave, or you never leave.*

And as I climbed down the scarp into the trees
Of this abated wilderness, a tropicbird dropped
From the canopy and played her wings across my face

> *Like sheet lightning across the night. Only cooler*

Than that. And her tail, softer than rain, as she fell,
And longer than love, felt like a sumptuous enactment
Of the first slow moves in a long seduction of farewell.

Late Spring Snow, Reno

THERE IS NOTHING so unbearable, so maddening, as the mystery
    Of material things, hiding themselves fast within their slow self-sufficient
Selves. Who are they really, the mountains of light, the spring's first

Precocious blossoms, the live oaks and gray squirrels, the alpine
    Meadows and graduate students and their books and laptops,
When they're alone in their beds? When they have no more use

For us? The senate of the sky has torn up all its books of lore
    And it rains them down like cold ticker on a scholars' parade,
Like every hope the world ever abandoned, all around the library.

I sit here three floors up in the tower and watch my mind at work
    Out there, in metaphor, while the afternoon fills with snow.
The more we know about matter, the more like mind

It becomes—the mountains, for instance, have disappeared
    Into the mountains in a matter of only minutes. And the afternoon
Flocking the windows on three sides of me is a strident one-act play

About the inner life of everything. Film noir in negative. Black
    And white without the black, and without the femme or the fatale
And with the sound turned way down low. The white pines

Beside the business school are chanting their name as if they meant it.
    And it looks more and more like they do. I had no idea the world
Had so much white to waste. Or so much silence to pronounce.

At my back the books hide out like category errors on their shelves, and I
    Sit and watch the molecular structure of my mood chase its tail
Through three dimensions on the other side of the glass. Between episodes

Of myself, these days, I fall apart, like weather, profligate and indeterminate,
    A million boundless ideas shopping aimlessly for a form to carry
Themselves home in. But mind like matter is never made up. Things

Are only fixed in our memories. On a beach somewhere a wave
    Of sleep passes like a sonorous tsunami, like a spring snow
Storm, through a flock of silver gulls. Somewhere else my children

Wake and you, love, think of me, as if I were what you used to think me
    And nothing between us were uncertain. And I think of you as if distance
Were an easy temptation to refuse. Meantime, the white voices of the dead

Chorale through what might well be the end of the day. The world lies
    About, reality flies about us, in its pieces. For all our art and fabulous craft,
We float helpless in the face of the uncanny and unfinished world.

Basin and Range

For William Fox

Someone's sleeping rough down there:
         the Great Basin torqued beneath me, as I fly
   Through fair weather across the solar plexus of America. This is how I sleep,
My rest a playa, my unrest a range, each night a flash-driven geomorphology
                of unrequited loss. My past lives
                        bidding for their inheritance.

This is how I wake; it's how I am. All my poise a fraud. The desert is a field
               of petrified twitches, stilled contortions;
   It wears its calm like a dress pulled tight over ancient grievance.
It rehearses impassioned discourses, 500 erotic moves,
                 at least, in the trim sage-gray effigy it calls sleep.

Grace

—Sheldon Museum of Art, University of Nebraska, Lincoln, 5 April 2011

T HE GALLERY's a temple of light on the polite east Nebraskan plain
  And its pillars look like the fossilized limbs
                         of two or three long-legged mammoths,
Caught by a sudden change in the climate somewhere in the middle
  Nineteen-sixties. The smallest sound fills it like water in a well.
                The clearing of my throat, a gunshot;
The scraping of my chair on the polished limestone floor, a sonic boom. I'm here to kill
  A shining spring hour before a class. Three centuries of still life are here
                     on the walls of the upper rooms of the Rain Gallery

To tend the poetical fire of the domestic moments they stole from time.
  When into this secular tabernacle of sound stumble
                   a dozen school children in the tumble of their holiday
Voices. A teacher shushes them and they stand in a blue semicircle under the copper vault
  And sing. Older in the wisdom of their articulations
                  than the sum of all their years; older
In the architecture of their utterance, than time—
                  a ring of children falls still and manufactures grace.
  "What'll I do," they sing in tight polyphony, "when I wander far,
                    and think of you? What'll I do?" The same question
                        the budding plum trees are putting to the sky.

Fifty Words (or more) for Snow

For Lise and Adrian

UNDER THE ICE, under the snow, under the night,
    The pike bide all our time. The waters wait.

The ice we stand beside disdains our listening's
    Bait. From the house, a hundred thousand

Phonemes rain; above, the dark translates a universe
    Of fire into the sound all silence makes. And all

Around the lake that was a glacier once and then
    A creek, the aspens quake and feel no need

To speak that one soft word the humans use
    To cover an awful lot of what lies at their feet.

Puck

1. Flash puck

THE CASEMENT window in the McDonalds at Pacific Central
Backs onto the park, but not a person in there is looking
Out. On six screens the Vancouver Canucks are tied at ones
With the devil (the LA Kings), and thirty-seven faces are tuned
In. The game is a slick and elegant brawl and the ball is an offcut
That moves faster than light, and the connotation of every flash
And feint and thick melee is lost on no one here, but me.
The commentary is an arcane discourse as slick as the puck
And the (sub) text transcribing it at the bottom of the screen
Is losing more ground than I am. Behind the slower screen,
To which I turn for solace, three tall trees move like shadow
Puppets in the half-light of three-quarter time. One, a chestnut,
I think, stands stilled by its own art, white blossoms festooned
In its hanging limbs, pale beads in its dark dreadlocks. The game
Ends badly for the Cannucks, and the faithful evacuate McDonalds
As if it were an emergency—everything that mattered as redundant
Now as cold fries and paper cups, so much rapid hunger unrequited.

2. Slow puck

And now I sit on the train thinking how little I know about love
After all these years and roadmiles. Thinking, waiting for the wheels
Of the world to turn again, I'm closing in on the end of the longest
Day of my life, a Sunday I started in one hemisphere and started
Again fifteen hours later in the other. Beside the track three games
Of soccer kick the covers off three blue balls under orange lights.
And on the mountain there are lights on the snow like the head-
Lamps of cars queued at a crossing. "Love is short," wrote one
Of the artists at the show I saw this afternoon, "but thinking about
Love never stops." Love never stays, but it never stops. And still
The train sits. "You can't make art till you remake yourself," wrote
One of the *automatistes*. Love remakes us by taking us apart. Most
Of me stays lost in the dark; I go looking with a pen, and what
I make is a hole the same shape as anyone's guess at who I am,
Where I've seeped through the blackwash. The train trembles
Softly and starts at last its four-day pilgrimage back the way
It came. On the pitch the soccer is still in flood, and, at the top
Of the mountain, the lights are still a logjam waiting to break.

The Wild Life of Southern Ontario: An Essay in Silence

THE TWO BEARS I didn't see; the three wolves
I thought I did; the coyotes that they probably
Were; the beavers at their profligate leisure
In a thousand lodges felled and formed
From the fastness of the forest; the bird
I could not name; the eagle that I could;
Something that ducked its head under
The black meniscus of the pond as the train took
The long causeway past; the crow and the raven
And their multitudinous clans; two Canada
Geese synchronizing watches and staying
Right on message in perfect silence as we rolled
Like thunder by.
                The only noise anywhere is the train.
And it's in the train: the lumbermen who climbed on board
In lace-up boots and safety vests, like bland bandits,
When we stopped at a level-crossing earlier,
And the young ones who've grown cabin-fevered
And taken over the car with beer and cards
And sexual innuendo have banished me
To the lounge, hungry for the kind of quiet
All the wildlife in southern Ontario
Are consuming out there in the woods
For free.
          On dusk, I watch two loons making all hell

Of a black and white racket on the other side
Of the glass, turning their backs on the wildness
Of the train's encroaching swagger and clang for
The uncompromising introversion of the trees, rising
In arpeggios of panic from one more of the ten
Thousand lakes that keep the original silence,
Like a memory of violence, in this timbered place
On earth.

Ontario Slides

1.

ONTARIO SLIDES past my window.
A red-tailed hawk—
Hungry, but not letting on—
Circles ploughed fields. Nothing knows
How to cast shadow today.
                              The black earth,
Turned, turns gray again in the sunlight, and mice
Run a furrowed gauntlet. Harvested
Wheat, a bad haircut all the way
To the horizon; the past laid
By in high-waisted barns, roofs
Applied like lipstick, walls like
Secondhand suits.
                        Spring greens the birches
And the ash, finishing a sketch
Winter had abandoned. Time kills
Time along the forest's edge. The afternoon
Hunts without intent, and Ontario walks
Backwards past my window,
Looking over its shoulder
Toward Toronto.

2.
I send you this poem by email. The things
One can do these days on a moving train—I sit
You beside me, my hand in your lap, my words
Out your window.
                   The woman in the seat
In front argues languidly with her boyfriend,
Or someone's boyfriend, on Skype. She's right,
I can tell, but being right
Rarely settles it; sometimes distance
Is the only thing that will.
                       Lake Ontario,
Like several small seas whose names have run
Together, lies out the lefthand window now, and
Thousands of miles away, you wake up
Tomorrow.

3.
We come among suburbs now
Where a city warehouses its other lives. Ontario
Stops, time finds its groove again, and the city starts
Up, but still the sun's not moved
A muscle since we set out.

Inside Passage, Sunday Morning

I WISH YOU WERE going where I am
                              going. But I take the Inside Passage
  Through Sunday waters, alone; the ferry freights
A thousand conversations east, and still, in all this bright noise,
  Most of what needs saying stays unsaid. Meantime
Morning washes the windows clear and sunlight falls in
  Love with the shadows it spawns everywhere, and words tumble like pigeons
                              through blue air. Divine sense swills the decks.

Off the starboard side a pod of killer whales
                              is looking for whatever shapely kind of trouble
  They can find. The spring sun steps out across the water,
And a dozen islands, bobbing about like temperate icebergs,
                              compose in loden green and grey basalt,
  A watercolour image of all the angels of one's wiser nature.
But the sea-spray draws a veil across whatever this drawn-out moment means,
  The land disappearing before one's very eyes—
                              back into the patient drama of its own possible life.

Halfway Home

Dawn breaks for three hours straight along the wing
Of a 747, six thousand miles behind me, two thousand

Miles to go, Pentecost Island like a small light off the tip
Of the port wing.
                    While I lay across three seats impersonating

Sleep, a whole day disappeared; it happens all the time. The sea
Is blue and legioned and steep with days, and it's fifteen hours

Across. The Pacific is an isobaric book of tides beneath
Me that has swallowed up where I've been.
                                    But as long as my watch

Tells me the time I left behind, I'm still halfway there: midday
Tuesday in Vancouver; five a.m. Wednesday in Sydney; no time

At all where I am, thirty-six thousand feet above Noumea.
You step into an airport near midnight and mountains fall

Away. Everywhere you've been, shut like a child's pop-up
Book, till the next time someone picks it up.
                                  Your old life

Ahead of you yet, waking without you; you're a thicket
Of afterthought, swimming home in high cloud.
                                        But home

Is a fable, too, from this height, and you hang stateless, Aeneas
On a string that no one holds. You're rowing home high in a medium

As mythic and elegant as Virgilian hexameter.
                                                Nearing home
Is like remembering the future, and you're hungry to make it

New this time, truer than how it's ever run before.
But everything of course—once one lands—

Will be much the way it was.
                              Nearing home,
You're a ghost walking out of rehab, stepping back

Into a body you cloaked while your inner life wandered
The peneplain; you're putting on old clothes now

At thirty thousand feet and trying to stand up in them again.
Dawn's still breaking hours later, when time starts to remember

Itself. History resumes, the sea resolves to come to an end; you tighten
Your belt and feel the plane relent.
                                      Home is an island

Below you now, clouds bivouacked along its eastern shore; home
Is a theatre of war in its own aftermath, and an army of other ghosts

Is massed there, waiting for the right wind
To carry them way back out beyond their depth.

Rain at Eltham

BETWEEN SHOWERS I stand on the deck not dying,
                talking to myself, saying stop talking to yourself.
  Saying: Come back and stand in the body of the present tense.
Drop down from the stream of twitter you use
                to remind yourself of everything you ever did wrong; remember
  The larger mind that makes you up. And at that point the sky decides
To haul up its net, and rain drops
  Cold from the crush of its seething catch like seawater,
                cold and black as Kali's eyes.

Spend your life dying. Take each step, make each clause,
                and every next move an act of willingness
  To die again. Turn up, in other words. But right now, come in out of the rain.
Which falls on the roof like a school
                of groupers ecstatic in escape and plunging willingly back
  To live again and again in the darkness. I sit where I sat a year ago
When the garden was a camp in the desert.
  This high room is crying out for a lover, but there's only me,
                and the room will just have to get over it.

The ironbarks, black as coal-seams in the rain, are in flower.
                         The one that weeps beside the deck sweeps its blue leaves
    Across my sightline. A lorikeet and a silvereye, voluble and garish circus acrobats,
Trapeze the tree's pendulous gesticulations
                         and swig in full swing sly grog from virtual pink plastic cups.
    The cloud frays and summer remembers itself in a few chaste phrases
Spilled across the shining deck. Borrowed light steals
    Slantwise through the eight panes of glass in the door
                         and falls like a sensual elegy on pale blond boards.

Along the River Tonight

A<small>LONG THE RIVER</small> tonight,
Wind among the sheoaks like petrichor.
An eagle flies lazy ellipses
Along the Razorback Ridge. Late light lies white
In the grasses there.
The voices of spinebill, wagtail, and bulbul.
I suppose the track is coming to know me now,
And walking here tonight
I might almost look as if I move without care.
I pass a mother and her child, I pass a man with his dog,
And I greet them, and they can't know I've come to shed
The day and slow my mind to the river's
Pace, slower than mine,
Its level lower than my mood.
Beside me as I run the river home: spinebill,
Wagtail, bulbul.

III—In *Medias* Res

Doing the Numbers: 02/01/2017

The two most important days of your life are the day you were born and the day you find out why.
—Mark Twain

For Steve Armstrong

      T OMORROW, for what it's worth,
       Is the day
        I once was born. This year I'm hoping to be born
    All over again. Summer has lost
      Its nerve and half my mind
     Is overcast. And I sit outside at my books,
Doing the numbers, a kind of numerological
    Stats: the year:
      $2 + 0 + 1 + 7$
Makes 10; and my years (a five and a five)
    Make another:

Ten. A twofold wholeness
          Last year (9 + 9)
Was never going to reach. The numbers won't
          Do it on their own, though; the work
                    Is all ahead of me and all
          Of it is mine. I am the sum of my years,
And more, and here's hoping I make them count. But wait:
          The day and the month
                    And the year make 13.
Not so good. But, no: I choose the happier reading.
          From now on

          I choose the brighter path,
                    The wiser way.
At breakfast in the hills, a single fallen leaf of mountain
          Ash lies, an impressionistic billabong,
                    Where it lay yesterday,
          An old leaf turning over a new year on the bench.
The past falls away to open a way for the future
          To leaf out. I read in the leaf, all
                    Its numbers up, an oracle:
Master the art of leaving. Fall, painted by your past, into the days
          That wait.

January Poplars

THE LEAVES of water poplars, demobbed angels,
   Rained down through January that year like all

The water the month withheld.
                              All January I read
   Outside in unrelenting light—cruel and glamorous

Hours, blue as heavens, sharp as glass, more
   Like worlds than days: for they had cost

The earth and travelled ages round it just
   To be here, and one could not begin

To spend them well enough.
                            We pay for our lives

   With our lives, making things, small worlds,
From nothing and leaving them behind, as if

   They mattered, as if it mattered that we'd been.
But it matters no more than the leaves matter

   And the trees they leave behind.
                               Late in the month,
An overnight storm, and in the morning the leaves,

    Felled by feckless rain the month had given up on,
Strew the ground like a vivid snow. It only

    Matters that we loved, that we forbore
Despair and left a few things better than they found

    Us. And in time the days will rain again and
The trees will recall what January is for.

Mecca

*I*F YOU THINK *you're in love, you're in love,*
Says the premier (of all people);
*If you think you're in traffic, you're in
Traffic.* Well, I think I'm in trouble.
I sit reading *The Bhagavad Gita* in Mecca,
The one on the corner of York Street,
And the gods are rolling my heart
Like a die down King. They're staking
My whole life. And something
Quite like traffic is banked at the lights

Outside the café, but I think it's going
To pass. In my dream I thought I was in India,
But I was only in a dream. In the bus
This morning, I thought I saw the loveliest
Girl in the world. But she was only in the bus.
And then she wasn't. But not everything passes,
Does it? Beauty, for instance? Time? I sip coffee,
And I turn the page, and Krishna asks me:
*How does this faint heart come to you? It is not
Heavenly, and it brings on disgrace. Let go*

Of this lowly weakness of the heart
And stand up. So I drain my coffee and stand up
Into the morning, which I see now is fierce
With contentment, and I pay my bill.
And I carry my two selves—the aging
And the ageless—upstairs, as if to battle,
And I get on with whatever this is
I'm supposed to be in.

Balmain Nocturne

IN TURNER STREET, at midnight, a dozen cars
                          have fallen asleep at the wheel.
   High in the frangipani a few lights burn—children reading late
In bed. The moon has overslept.
   Bending its head, the lemon-scented gum forgives everyone almost everything.
The blooms of the jacaranda at the top of the street are just

The kind of shadow the night
                          would cast if it could. And way up
   In their dark heavens, a thousand suns burn
The candle at both ends, working overtime
   To be the stars in our sky. Alone at night, I am wide awake
In my other life, translating the unsayable world.
                          Language only seems to be

For making sense. Words are not for telling
                          things, but for joining them
   In the perpetual recreation of the real. And you, my love,
Who can ruin a man's day with a word
   And make his night with a glance, throw off all doubt, miles away,
In sleep, and lie dreaming
                 in the dialect of flowers.

With Sarasvati Under the Lemon-Scented Gum Tonight

M OST OF THE TIME I show up
                in my life as if it were a part time job. But tonight
  I sign on. Tonight, I walk deep into mid-November and let the half moon
Find me. Venus turns and gives me the eye.
                Live like you're going to die in the night, she says.
                              Like you won't be around to find out. How true you came

    Is all the trace you'll leave. How much you gave up
Is all you'll take with you. Love is not a trade; it's not a prayer;
                        it's not an answer. It's a question—posed
  Tonight by four arms and a tiny waist and plucked on a seven-string lute.
                                The world, her sharp perfume: there's your answer.

Blues Point Blues

L ATE LUNCH in light rain—
        the afternoon performs
                        her joyless striptease to a distracted house.
  Shiva sits in Billi's with a Spanish omelette and a book, and beside him
A thousand ephemeral streams ease south.
                    He rests thus in shrink-wrapped al fresco solitude,

  While the gutters run
                with traffic, and Kali lies upstairs, sleeping off
Her savage choreography. His mystic guile has danced her down this once.
  And a red Hardware & General truck lumbers uphill,
                rattling the post-coital calm
                        along Blues Point Road.

The Cycles of the Moon

New Moon One

EVENING now, the darkness just beginning
   To tell, and low above the paddocks, where
The kite was up early getting the hang
   Of herself again in the sallow morning light,
Going nowhere very fast;
                low above the paddocks
   Where a tractor winnowed felled grass
Into flight paths around noon,
                and the purple
   Heron flew them slowly home,
A brand new moon hangs, shyly now,
   Barely five percent of full.
                Cloud hides her,
But she's up there (bedding down), for sure.
   I have to take her on faith. For you see her,
A sly wink, you tell me—a suggestive slit
   In the old sky—where you sit by the sea.

New Moon Two

THE MOON fills with sorrow
   the sail of the beloved's
brand new ketch.

New Moon Three

THE NEW moon is a peach,
   Most of it a bruise: all you can see
Is the bite, smiling
   In recollection: How good she tasted
In his mouth. How much
   More there is to come.

New Moon Four

AH, there she is now:
   The ivory boat rocking
The wintering sky.

Full Moon in May

THE MOON is a searchlight tonight
                         trained on a peaceable sky.
  The first full moon of winter shines as bright
As a Broadway musical
                         and the middle distance looks like opening night.

She comes up out of aspens now
                         like the beloved out of a bath. At first, the first
   Full moon of winter is the biggest spotlight you ever got caught in;
But in no time, really, she's become a lamp by a child's bed.
                                  And by nine, she's way more *OM* than *omen*. Amen.

Peregrine Moon

            O NE SATURDAY afternoon in June, a peregrine flew east
                Across the window
                        Of the room where I stood teaching—preaching,
Probably—and turned all my talk to stone.
                        Sleek pilgrim, idling through the sacred
      In behind the beach, she trimmed the tops off the teatree scrub;
         Waking a quick and quiet terror indistinguishable
From the awe she'd expect to strike on any other sunstruck Saturday
Among New Holland honeyeaters, bluewrens and finches,
                    And (lower down the scheme of things)
       The echidnas, she carried on spreading the bright blue word softly
              Over everything. And so it was,
          The fastest being anywhere brought on the longest
                Night of the year,
           And pulled heaven about as near

        To earth as heaven may hope to come. And late the next day,
                The year's nadir
            Passed, the peregrine packed and gone,
One's bed made, some miles put between then and now, the perigee moon
        Came up, unfashionably early, above the city—the Buddha
            In a bathrobe. Fat-bellied trappist, she floated up
        Out of the river, thinking her one yellow and immemorial thought.
For a while she stood as close and still
                    As the moon ever stands, teaching proximity
                        By proxy,
Non-attachment by touch. And (in time) go.
            Ah, how one aches, though, for such slow propinquity;
                Love is the distance one sometimes closes down, a gap
                      That even now the moon is up there
                        Sliding wide again.

Guru moon

JUST LOOK at her up there now: chaste wastrel, what was she thinking,
   Flying so high with so little on? She's the beloved in flagrante, showering
               her whole self nakedly down
Over all of us—you and me, for instance, in our broken bits
                          and pieces, and over everyone else
We might have been and might yet, and
   Her ecstatic silence is so very like the love
               one had been standing here on Darling Street
Hands in one's pockets through all eternity,
             hoping to overhear a hint of. Outside your place,

Though, the wind has brought down two nests; it's dropped them,
   Two heavens, like bombs, on the path, and I cannot say how it is I know
               these are the nests of the two birds in the old Sanskrit yarn,
The singer and the sung. The self and the Self. And will she
            also shine, your pretty moon, you ask me,
                        down on these small vagrants of the world?

For the moon, though she governs like a goddess up there,
   Dispenses such a slim and forsaken, meagre refuge here.
                 Half the world is unhoused tonight, and words
Will not see them home. The evening is cold. The moon is growing distant.
               And down every street, old lovers are shutting their doors
                       and climbing old stairs to bed.

Yours Tonight

I NEVER SAW such a moon as the one I saw tonight, rising—as if it wasn't rising at all really, as if she were a lover after love—out of the floodplain, three nights past full into a band of blue cloud. I called my son outside to see. "What colour is it?" he kept asking. "Can't you see it?" I said. "What colour would YOU call it?" "But is it red or is it orange?" the boy said. "Who can say?" I said. "Must we choose? It's the colour it is." But the boy was right, and I wish I'd said so. The moon was Ruby, halfway out of her red dress. There should be one word, only one, for such a moon, for the look on her face. Someone had surely just told her she was the most beautiful being he had known on earth (or above it, as it were), and her colour, two degrees above the cold hills, is what it looks like to hear that, and always did.

This is how it is to "stand in love's sight", as Sharon Olds puts it. And there should be one turn of phrase for such a moon and the light that falls from her, and they should teach it in school; there should be one, and only one, metaphor. There should be lore. There must be a story. There must be a god. It makes you yearn, such a moon, rusted like the hinges on your best friend's side gate back when you were young, yellow as the rose petals thrown on happy and unhappy couples alike in a churchyard by the sea; it takes you back, such a moon, somewhere you've never been. It makes you ache for who you are and where you stand. It wants a name. *Let it be yours tonight.*

A Death in the Family

DRIVING HOME after teaching in the city, the moon waning above me, the stars a (holy) mess, the night asleep and dreaming up this very moment, and summer failing the way summer does about now each year, I listened again, inside my white car, inside the night and all its smoggy black matter, among the million reckless B-Doubles, to Dawn Upshaw singing Samuel Barber's lullaby "Knoxville: Summer 1915", a setting for voice and strings of James Agee's spontaneous prose poem, a lost childhood recalled and made over into all of our childhoods in ninety minutes flat back in 1948.

I pulled over, and, letting the traffic go on ahead, I googled, as one does, beneath the moon: "Knoxville", a third of which Barber uses in his alchemical rearrangement—a small undeceiving of the world, a musical disinterment of the poem within Agee's uncanny prose—became in time the introduction to a novel, *A Death in the Family*, a book of loss that Agee died finishing, a book that won him the Pulitzer two years too late. (For him.) "A near-perfect work of art," Amazon tells me "... that contains one of the most evocative depictions of loss and grief ever written." Perfect, I thought, for the chapter I'm writing on grief, the one that follows love, in a memoir of a life lived in sentences, to which I've promised myself to return this year, before my sentence ends.

Home was only thirteen degrees when I stepped out into it at ten, a sudden death, an other world, and the air smelled of creeks and sleeping children and probably stars, and inside, over soup at the breakfast table, I ordered two copies of *A Death*: a paperback to work with and a hardback, an "acceptable" 1957 copy, retired from a California library, to keep. For a work of art, if it's sad and perfect and broken and made of mind and speech, will need a body to walk it into its vernacular afterlife, and a good jacket in which to wait its grief out, and console us in ours, page after page.

Flash Fiction

So THE PHONE rings and it's a girl in pajamas sitting by the freeway smoking cigarettes she gave up months ago and she tells me how she loves a poet who doesn't really love her because poets are better at writing it than doing it; and she tells me that the man she's been seeing and whom she was working up the energy to fall for has just gone home to his wife and probably won't be coming back, and she suggests I never fall in love with anyone who isn't free to love me back or anyone who can talk about love and write about love and even make love quite nicely but who's scared to death of love because they don't know how to give themselves away because they don't know who the fuck they are, and she suggests I don't fall in love for instance with anyone like her, but she knows I know that's not what she means or why she called me from the freeway in her pajamas in the ten o'clock rain.

Three Shadows

IF I HAD A LOVER, I'd tell her this: The night where I am, cupped in hills, the day's heat dimmed, Christmas just over the ridge, is much too pretty not to share. Here's some of it: me out the back of my terrace, walking in old jeans and a white linen shirt, smoking a cigarette and watching three shadows of myself cast on the concrete by lights burning inside my house at 11:17, and the scent of pasture and summer in spate, thinking about what freedom might mean when all one seems to know is obligation and addiction and fatigue, and thinking it might mean such a night as this and no one to stop your stepping out into it and finding words for it and saying them or leaving them, like this, unsaid, and wondering what love might mean beyond the platitudes of this time of year, and thinking it might mean carrying the battle against tall odds and holding dear those who cannot hold you dear and practising kindness when all one feels some days is hurt; and if you can, think of me, love, here now walking a life like none I've been asked to live before, passing through childhood again to learn the old language of these new days and beginning shyly to believe I can parse its grammar and come to the end of its sentences and walk free into a language of days in which more than pain plays; and I'd like you, my love, to feel this breeze that wakes now where it lay all day at the feet of these pastured hills, a breath so soft and sleek it's like a silk of forgiveness inside the shimmer of delight, and feel with me how it finds me here, among the shadows of my three selves, which walk with me like children on the eve of Christmas. And the crickets sing and a few cars pass and lightning swells in the distance like a bright wound or a lamp in the window of a fishing shack on some far shore where the other end of this December night washes up.

Disappearance

       E<small>VERYTHING</small>,
It appears, disappears.
We spend our lives
Losing our grip on our time here, whatever
We thought that was for—and we were for—within
A life's span. Living feels like practising
Ahead of the main event, which never comes: each day
Another increment
In our coming to an end,
Each minute another
Downpayment on the price
We pay for getting to be here
At all.

Everything
Is always on its way
From somewhere
To somewhere else. Each place, for instance,
Always becoming some place else; the past, some other past;
The weather a problem always too far out
To fix. Morning passes
Into afternoon, May into June. One minute,
I'm in preschool, the next
I'm outside the dementia ward. The whole middle
Ground a disappearing
Act. If only it were
An act.

The Last Day

THREE ELMS STAND bright as bauxite against purple snow clouds.
                Someone has dipped the trees
            In ink the very colour of desire. But three minutes on,

Their small moment past, the trees slump in the dusk. The cloud rolls north.
                The hill to the east, though,
                    Is violet yet, and the clouds above it are mauve and yellow and grey.

The end of things, like the start, is often electric. 5.35 today: an essay in love
                And grief, so often paired,
                    In my experience—delight and fear, tenderness and panic.

What made me look up to see this? The useless world consoles
                Even when one's lost
                    In one's self, one's several incoherent selves, one's industry. The world

Flares. Beauty insists on itself; night insists on itself after that. And just as it does,
                This day, a kookaburra cants
                  And the violin slides like a lover in fresh sheets all the way down to the end

Of the partita. I seem to have forgotten how to live my life. Something in me
                Wants just one god,
                  One muse or another, the tree or the cloud. Magenta or cyan. Darkness

Falls: why, still, can I not bring my heart to rest like that? The world is neither right
                Nor wrong. It is dusk, and then
                  It's midnight, then dawn. All there is, is earth, this single manifestation

Of eternity. And all one has to do is live, in joy and in woe. Perhaps in praise. And yet,
                       Offered two heavens,
          I want only one. But which one? Did anyone else ever die of delight?

Tonight the moon is new again, shy as you were. She is an empty boat above the city
                       In the pale estuary
            Of dusk. In her—nothing but beauty and longing. And something I let slip.

Body Copy

I HAVE an exile heart,
                and my mind is unfaithful
    To everything it loves. My body is too slender
To contain my life. So lend me yours.
                          Let me take you,
    Now and then, like a pilgrimage.
But only if you take me, too.
                    Above the reservoir

    This morning the snowgum,
                    old enough to know better,
Puts out a new shoot from an old wound,
    Into the resurrected light
                of late October.
Four pelicans swim the divine
    Dichotomy slowly across the discontented shallows.

On the path bluewren busies
                himself on his blackberry
    With a life he doesn't know
How not to lead. In the Paddy's River box trees
    Firetails are stripping assets
From a tired enterprise they picked up in the crash.

    The track is a random walk
                between honeysuckle and hawthorns,
An absent-minded choreography
   Of hope. I am everywhere but here,
And you are nowhere else.
                  Draw yourself from your bath
   Tonight and stand and think of me,
                    water dropping from your body

Like nothing in particular. Then slip back
                    into the tub again,
   Like the moon into the morning.
Let me live beyond my body's means,
                way beyond the reach of my faith-
   Ful heart. Let me try on everything
I love. This morning, for instance, the lake.
                   Tonight, maybe you.

In Medias Res

I WOKE
THIS MORNING in the poet's dark wood, right
in the middle of my own bright putative life. The straight way
was lost, and the woods weren't lovely, but they were sure
as hell dark and deep. And if there were promises to keep,
I hadn't kept them, not in the hours of sleep, not in all the years
before, and I woke with the taste of fire, at least I think it was fire,
in my mouth and the words in medias res on my lips.

I think
WHAT I MEANT was nel mezzo del cammin di nostra vita, but Dante's
Italian had collapsed into Horace's Latin overnight in the heat
of the improvident bonfire of my dreams, and all the water
had drained from the lake of my heart, beside which I'd been
camped. And the thick of it is where it always tends to start,
no matter what language you want to start in, and starting—no matter how
fearful you feel, no matter how lost the straight way—is all there is for it.

I was
THE UNBEARABLE kind of lonely you get to be when your body's there,
but you yourself are not, and when you wake beside your lover,
your three children strewn like the promises, perhaps, you forgot
to keep, across the floor of the selva oscura, which had until recently
been your bed. And I know you'd like to hear me say

I scattered
THE CHILDREN toward breakfast and let my beloved fuck
me slowly true again, but that's another poem. And it seems I'm stuck
in the middle of this one for now, and miles to go
before I wake. I'm not complaining, or not too loud,
but every morning I have to make myself up again, remember
myself at the desk, stop and regather the atrophic pieces of who
perhaps I am beside the road that's new each time I take it.
I don't find any of this easy to understand, but it's like this: I have

two lives,
AND WHENEVER I turn my back,
my small life resumes the colonisation of the big life I lead
on the side. I crowd myself out of who

I might be.
MY BIG LIFE feels small then, caged
—a farm dog in a terrace-house, a panther in a zoo—
most of itself lost to its self in the artificial wilderness of appearances to be kept
up. It paces, trying to remember the moves, trying not to surrender,
trying to keep the future in its sights, trying to see the wood again for

the trees.

Catullus, at Dusk, Lustful and Heartbroken, Tries His Hand at Haiku

YOU crashed my house. You
   Smashed my household gods. So where
Am I now you've gone?

Shreds

THE MORNING is two lives at once,
                           a neap of blue light stilled between two tides:
One life I'm getting used to, after;
                           the other I'm getting used to
Having had. The morning is nowhere I've been or hoped to be; it's a mild blues
                        impression in the present perfect tense.
And I sit with it gravely over coffee in the lane behind the school. The morning's
Up too early to throw shadows with me
                       on the street; and the wind's altogether too unused
       To where it finds itself to blow.
                The morning's forlorn as a tree
Without a wood. It waits like a memory of mornings it once was,
Unsteady yet for futures it foretells.
                       It's the child's happy cry beside me in his pram, his mouth
An oral history of crusts; it's his mother's proud apology, her smile.
                                   The morning is a hundred
Pages stripped by children from a hundred
                      long-suffering paperbarks, along a creek;

        A dozen lapsed and overlapping sentences,
                their syntax shot, their soundings silenced,
Forty-two lines on the subject of nature and loss, scrambled by recent events,
Looking without much hope for a new paragraph
To call home. And now the morning comes
                 and parks its truck across
My point of view: *Shred It* say the letters on its side.
                    Shred it: shed all the grief the morning

        Cries; shred all the other days, the reasons why, the old
Accustomed ways, the ghosts and opportunities, it casts;
Dispose thoughtfully
            of how you thought you went
And how you'd go from here. Tear the god-
Damned morning down; pull out all the broken teeth
                    from all the broken smiles;

        Trash all the pretty promises the past made
            in its sleep; piece all improbabilities together
Again, and call what they make what you will.
Call it a day. Call it tomorrow.
               Take all the cobalt pieces in which the morning makes
Your new face up. Take your shredded, watershedded days
And nights, your fallings short, your oversights,
                and call them the rest of your life.

Youth: A Second Coming

THE TROUBLE IS, the joy of it: you never spent
    Your youth; you never misspent it, anyway.
You've been saving it up. And by now, its returns
    Somewhat diminished, it's earned you a deal

Of interest. Entering now your fifty-eighth year—
    Closing on your sixth decade—you feel about
Ready to withdraw; to waste without haste the youth
    You knew even then would have been lost

On you; you were much too old in those old
    Days, and serious, to have entertained
Much interest in playing your way to the edge
    And, who knows how or when, back again.

But, wasted now, yourself, (just a little) by time
    And weather and trouble, you feel ready
To forget the rules and find, maybe, that second
    Freedom the more worldly scriptures

Speak of. Moth flight; leaf clamour. The holy
    Embrace of the trees. The grove. Perhaps
The dryads, shapely attendants of one's loneliness.
    The tenderness. The slenderness. The road,

On which you'll meet yourself, a second time,
　　Coming back the other way. And maybe you'll
Choose to sit with yourself in the lap of the trees and
　　Weep. Ready for the game just as the game

Ends, centuries ago. You'll sit there, certainly, unlearned,
　　And unfinished, ready like a shadow, steady
Like the sunlight, to fall—for though it was sometimes
　　Much too early, it never was really too late.

Fish Me Up Plural

T HE DAY is raining
    As if it hoped to fill
  An emptiness as deep
As I have fallen into.

      The rain is writing
  Down every word
    I can't draw up
This morning from the deep

      End of July.
So let the rain
    Drown me all the way
Down to the belly of the tides
               and fish me

      Up plural, as Rumi
  Puts it—awake
    (Again) with many lives,
And other times.
         Among them,

     Yours; among yours,
  Mine. The day is a net
    Through which all worlds
Run like longing.
         In which

   Only love is caught. And
  Among its catch, species
    Of every school of standing—
Beginning again, like this—

    In rain that does not begin
  To know how to stop
   Being everything
The world is and everything
     It once loved.

IV—Bach, Or Is It *Ravel?*

At Night the House

AT NIGHT the house throws
                bright shadows over everything
  That was so hard by day. My own shadow
Reaches out long and dark and thin,
                        barnacled with frog song, toward the river,

    As if it had forgotten my way home. The length of one's wanting, I know, is the length
Of one's unhappiness. My life is rich and round, and I'm coming apart
    Trying to keep it together. So it goes. Flick the switch:
                                        call your shadow home.

Bach, Or is it Ravel?

For Rachel Marks

Y̲OU WAKE at four, the hour
                it seems the dead change shifts.
  You walk without clothes into the tepid predawn to calm the dog,
And from the house behind you two notes sound
                          on your grandmother's piano,

    Where no one sits. Bach, you think. Or is it Ravel?
                          Some hymn. A pavane
Runs its chromatic fingers up your spine. There's a music out there that plays us
    All by heart, but two notes, a hint of a chord, is all
                    you'll ever know of the hand that plays it
                                  or the score.

Self Portrait

T HE FACE in the mirror, as she cuts
                my hair, is not the face my writing wears.
  Strange to rise from days at a desk, where I am
A voice fashioning a self from syntax,
                        putting the world together again

  In thought—and see myself sitting there
                        in time again at half past four, my hair falling
Like years to the floor. I see a man restored to history
  And genealogy, biography even,
                    but not improved by it. Not especially.

Casting Shadows in Early April

T HE DAY AFTER Easter, and the weather
                looks like everything
   The scriptures had advertised. The wind's been up,
Talking in tongues—two of them, at least,
                            south by southeast—since sunrise;

   The message isn't simple, but it's very, very clear. And the afternoon light
Has arrived from everywhere at once
                            to remind you how to stand and throw a shadow
   Long and clean and way beyond the ambit of the empty moment
                                        this had seemed till now.

Your Voice

Y OUR VOICE, saying my name, is the beach
                when I first catch sight of it, down
    Through the scribbly gums, nursemaids of this quiet light; your voice, an infidel,
Lies almost untouched—and, there, untouched again—

    By the pale water, which is time. And time again. Your voice,
                                      a mare's hoofprint winnowed
By onshore gales, has been waiting for me beyond the trees,
    Sitting in the ocean's lap, hoarding light and silence, and listening
                                    for my syllables to arrive and step
                                                into the soft hollow of its longing.

Windfall

P EARS LIKE vivid artillery shells
        lie unexploded in the grass,
  And more rain falls. Bowerbirds inspect the damage:
Bomb disposal experts with a death wish.
                Crimson rosellas, flashy auditors, pick

    Over the fallen fruits as if they were dislodged tax returns. Opening my dictionary
In search of *windfall*, I walk, instead, into the *Wind River Range*
   And in four syllables I am back there with you,
                watching the day bank a fire under heavy cloud.

The Geography of the Middle Distance

SEVEN PELICANS eat the sky
              and carry it away, awkward in flight
  As Pontiacs in traffic, late light glancing their fenders
And falling to the ground. Ghosts graze the middle distance,
                        neither here nor there: ground we can never gain.

  I'm sure that ecotone beyond the hedge is where the departed pasture,
Waiting till at last we see the whole
                way through the tenuous material
                        world, where all our hopes mill
  Myopically, pretending not to look out or back
                  from behind their terribly fashionable reflective sunglasses.

So Little to Say, So Much Space to Say It In

WINTER is the silence
         you nearly killed yourself
    Trying to finance. But when it comes at last, as it does again this morning,
It's always just a little more silent than you'd meant. Way too much

     Elsewhere and *otherwise* enameled on the sky's tin cup.
                                 And then there's the problem of your self,
Sitting here, a chipped glass in your hand and more water swilling
    In the flask than you'll get to the bottom of by spring,
                                and no one anywhere to drink to.

The Propinquity of Snow

IT'S COLD HERE, though the wind has died
               down with dusk. All day
   You could smell the propinquity of snow in the blueness of the light.
The year is at its nadir, and winter is burning

   Every log it laid by through summer
               for just such a night as this. The fire
Is a weary dance of veils behind me; the dog has fallen fast asleep
   All over the kitchen floor; and the night wants to go on forever.

November Rain

EARLY NOVEMBER. Heat builds
        like hope. And ends
    Like mercy. This morning a soft rain works hard
To put out the lights that burn in summer's bed—starflower
                                and foxglove and rose, a profligacy of grace,

A trespass of beauty—so that afternoon might come
                            along and turn them on again.
Remembering is my morning's work; my afternoon's, forgetting.
    But with luck, the magpie larks will play me right through to the close,
                                music like your garden bed, lyrics like the rain.

Landscape with Laptop

A<small>ND THE LAPTOP</small> sits there like a metaphor
                    in the morning. The table
    Where it rests used once to be a barn door; now it's a floodplain
In middle age, and its paint peels like stray bids, like old words fallen
                                    overnight out of fashion. Spasmodically,
                                        the leaves of the water poplar touch

    Type the morning's memoir on the sky;
                    inspiration's such an unreliable affair. Nothing moves
The laptop, though. Its attitude is yogic; its screen a tabula
    Rasa upturned. Shadows swarm it like a clamour of starlings; crowds
                            gather; clouds pass; but still the Air finds
                                            nothing apt to utter.

V—Break & *Enter*

I Ran So Far

I RAN so far because the beach was so long, and you
                Were at the end of it.
When I passed the trespass sign, I recognised my enterprise, and ran on.

At the lagoon, where the sea's edge was steeped in whatever
                It is that steeps
Old photographs, I turned, and started back. The surf turned, too,

At that point, lay on its back and admired its reflection
                In the foxed blue
Mirror of the sky. The wind carried the morning away east, and the body

Of the beloved lay ransacked along the tideline—
                Bladderwrack, man-o-war,
Deadman's fingers, Neptune's toes—and if my legs began to feel

My age, carrying me home, I couldn't say: all pain
                Passes thus,
Transfigured into the way the distance sees straight through you

As you come; transposed into the steady (now) rhythm
                On the sand
Of your slow return into that first place you left so long ago.

Among Trees

I HAVE COME among trees
As if among friends; and between the trees and me a light
Rain falls like a conversation dropped one day
One hundred years ago. Today we pick it up
And share it like fruit, and light leaks from the words like gravity, and
The place falls still. The trees make all the silence
There ever was to make. There are as many
Troubles in the world
As there are leaves fallen on this forest floor (so many books returned unopened),
And dusk settles on each of them in turn. In last light, the marri shed

Bodies it seems they only wear
To hold the daylight up—and step near. Memory becomes birdsong;
Green becomes grey; grey becomes every colour
On the wheel. Each car that passes
Along the wet road below pixelates this almost perfect picture of the truth
And rights it again. There's civil war in Syria, and cyclones
In Sri Lanka; in Canberra the tax-base has collapsed;
And everywhere the CO_2
Is piling up like evidence. The trees, though, breathe out their accustomed ease,
In which I set a candle down and wait for nothing much at all.

I eat an apple. Hours pass. You call me
In. Rain falls and lifts, falls and lifts, on the house of the beloved. We make,
Later, a furious love, you and I, the kind that rebirths
Selves and strips the leaves off
All wanting. Later still, rain crashes our sleep the way Dante crashed Hell,
And we are all the hope that he abandoned. It is ten o'clock, and
It is midnight, and it is two. But time does not pass
Here. It gathers (like shade)
And takes root. It becomes a forest and grows new again. It becomes a long contentment,
Full beyond words. Earlier than everything. It becomes a day of rain.

Fog Lies...

L IKE A SIMILE (of blessing withheld),
                above the parched and apostate lake. In the lay-bys
   Elms and poplars reprise their eternal fiery thing.
And the rain is the morning's small talk over coffee.
    Leaves fall like clichés—some ancient; some modern—on the picnic tables between.
And the ridge, that beautiful contusion in my soul,
                rises south by southwest into the crooked and incontinent
   Sky. This is where my life makes sense, especially in the fog.
          When there's a whole lot less
                    meaning to get in the way.

Fog hides out like rogue sheep in the teatrees
                      by the road, performing its holy trickery:
   Making the invisible world visible, coagulating silence.
It drowns the day at birth, and it ghosts the other world
                      into being, incarnating the theoretical and obfuscating
   The real. Fog articulates all the inarticulate spaces
Within the sinuous syntax of the here and now all the way along the long road south.
   It makes consonants of all the vowels in the morning's mouth.

Further along, it drops into the valley
                of the river Yass,
                              and ransacks the daylight's drawers.
  It splays all her lascivious lingerie across the bottom-
Lands and paddocks and pulls them taut across the buttocks
   Of the ridge. It declares the secret devices the dawn employs
              in ordinary time to entrap feckless romantics like me.
Like some inebriate moth, coming home in the small hours from the pub,
   I can make out every web for 280 ks,
                            but I can't see the road in front of me.

One AM Sublime

1.

STREETLAMP washes the empty road. You stand
At the gate and watch nothing pass. It's cold out,
A few degrees, no wind, plover cries, ice rings

The moon. In the distance, southwest, you hear
A sigh rise that could be the sea but isn't. Frogs
Chant heaven in the ditch, and possums grunt

Like vicars in the winter trees. One car, a second,
Passes. Your family sleeps. Love sleeps with God
Somewhere on the other side of the veil. Draw

Down slow on a cigarette and breathe your solitude
Out into another early morning of the current world.

2.

EARLIER still, you had watched the moon rise yellow
From the plain. You won't know that old peace

Again. Ah, but it doesn't matter; nothing ever was
As simple as you'd read. You feel strong in the night
Air, capable of exquisite silence. Inside again, the boy

Wakes: I couldn't find my gun he says in sleepy syllables.
You arm him and carry him back across the border.
Your neighbour has grown old and ill; lights burn

In her empty house. Do some good, you say
To yourself; lie down; sleep. You have been given
All this, and beauty never did come cheap.

Poem on Maundy Thursday

1.

As I DROVE past last night—
                abandoning the city, chasing the holiday's tail—
  Sunset was painting the original Fauvist landscape
All over the airport, grounding every flight beneath
                an apocalyptic gouache. But I sank, then, with the traffic,
  Underground, and by the time I surfaced, the show was over,
                      and the sky was another era,
Another oeuvre, altogether. In which the moon hung exquisitely,
  The last—overripe—fruit in the bowl,
                and the constellations were a mold spread over all eternity.

2.

If I believed in anything
              more than the weather, I could believe
  That Jesus himself would die for weather like this morning's and rise
Again and believe he'd gone to heaven.
  The beloved is cruel sometimes and contrary. Manipulative, even.
But it's only because she hurts. And this is how she hurts:
                the pain of unmitigated beauty, Dresden blue,
  Peerless, and strained to breaking across the first day of April,
            as far and long as death, as merciless as lust.

3.
The mountain stepped right out of her skin
                                         overnight, and I found her standing—
    Catatonic, ecstatic—on the corner of Station Street this morning.
It's eleven, now, and I'm back home, and there's a fire burning in the stove,
    And outside the wind is raising bubbles in the glass surface
Of the day. I walk out and look up
                           and see that he—or perhaps it's she—really has risen,
    A day or two early, admittedly:
                        a sea-eagle, in starched vestments, cruising cruciform,

4.
Practises stillness and self-
                        abnegation 1500 feet up in the polyphonous
    Cobalt vault of Lent. I take aim and shoot,
But my gaze only grazes her side, and she doesn't come down;
    She never does. Night falls, though, later,
                           and as it falls, I watch a kookaburra,
A bird that doesn't know how to miss, take a mouse
                                that makes one move too many
    A little too far from home. Life is death's aftermath; the afterlife
                          Of hunger; and the world will be back tomorrow, for sure.
                              Tomorrow or the next day.

At Home on a Sunday Trying to Find Nothing to Do

1. HANGING ON…

A COMMA is to a poet, of course, what a breath is to a yogi, and for much
The same reason. And the morning looks like she's breathing easy enough,

So I sit beside her at the table that used to be the barn door and which—
Unhinged these days, but slimmer—rests up near the house doing nothing

Perfectly well in all kinds of imperfect weather, and I try to find nothing
To do. Wearing today his proper name and raiment, the blue-winged king-

Fisher lands on one of the tired and sanctimonious digits of those Sad-
Ducees, the silver poplars by the cowshed. He takes a moment to reset

His moral compass then turns and throws me a look as stern as a line
From one of my grandfather's sermons. The wind swells like a chord

From a small pipe organ in the temple of the word, and the bird flies
To his pastoral work across the thirsty catchment of the Wingecarribee.

I could get out the gear, I guess, and roll another coat of whitewash
On the ceiling of the shed; I could make another run at the examined life.

But now, above me in the Osage Orange, a single sulphur-crested
Cockatoo, white as a lie, prim as a spinster, pins down one ripe green fruit

Like prey. She sips the acrid latex as if it were sweet tea and swallows
Half the flesh she flenses from the body. The other half she showers down:

So many post-it notes peeled from so much perfect body copy. Soon I'll be
Walking those second thoughts inside on the soles of my unknowing boots.

2. ... WHILE LETTING GO

THE MORNING, though, sits comfortably in her skin. A little light haze in the east
Is the least you'd expect in the wake of a night like last. Did the stars move

For you, too, my love? The white moths are out shopping early. One buzzes
A yellow dandelion and sucks at speed and slows and pivots and spies her mate

By the hedge and flies to him, as though she were in no kind of hurry at all,
And she's fooling no one but herself. I could kiss you on the mouth and see

Where that got us, if you were not half way home already. And I could start
To miss you, if I hadn't started that in the beginning. Or I could sit and watch dust

Rise and run north–south, ahead of a tractor down the back. Time to harrow
The fallow field and plant the winter crop. Time to lay one's thinking down

In windrows. But let me fix some breakfast first; that feels like work I'm
Good for. Some juice we made from some apples we picked, some eggs

The hens might have laid, if the foxes had not laid them waste first. Some ham
Off the bone of a beast I wouldn't know how to raise or kill or cure. But, hey,

I know how to drop it in some virgin oil and pull it out brown and wash it
Down with coffee I know how to brew on the stove. Everything, everywhere

Knows what to do. And when to leave it undone. Even I, when it comes to mind
To breathe, can sometimes sit, unmade a while, and let the morning come.

April into May

1. *How to know you're home*

Down in the paddocks the place
Makes the only poem it knows
How to make, and this afternoon,
Like every afternoon, I hear
The same poem I've never heard
Before. This afternoon, I hear
A yellow poem that smells of
Fallen poplar leaves and tastes
Like immigrant rain and moves
In slow dactyls like a god, a macro-
Pod tired of the dance, and
It looks like the last day of April.

*2. There is a fire resting
under the clouds tonight*

Down by the river, the light's
Getting into exactly the kind
Of trouble you'd like to get
Into yourself. The kind Orpheus
Got into: love and all of her
Killing, regenerative cadences.
And I think those might be his
Limbs I see down there plucking
The last notes of autumn from
The mouth of the easterly wind:
Love, that spendthrift, spending
Herself to a standstill in the silver
Trees, the sky threatening to fall.

3. Just who is reading whom?

On the pillow in the blue bed-
Room, the book lies face down,
Dreaming its own story all over
Again. The woman who sat
Through the afternoon reading
Has put the book down to walk out
And stand on the balcony and watch
The world, the untold world,
Become a word on fire, a word
She knows she must hold in her
Hands till it becomes her own
Name. Each tree, she thinks,
Is lonely in the flood of dusk
For the forest it might have
Been. Three black cockatoos,
Morning in their tails, mourning
In their mouths, close the day down
Deftly among the spangled timber
And open the reader like a book.

4. *The interregnum*

Five king parrots, their colours
Running, bunch in the water
Poplars to wait out the rain.

5. *Resurrection haiku*

I am full of poems
This morning: an Easter wind
Rises and dies again.

6. *Like this*

After reading some poems by Jane Kenyon and Mark Strand

In three years I've not sat once
On the back step like this in the sun
And read. For two years at least
I've been running. One morning

In late April I stop. But the world
Does not. Maples yellow along
The fence. Fair weather cumulus, spread
As thin as brittlegums in the desert,

Trawl south. Bluewrens flock
And forage. White moths stick
Their fingers in the till. Winter grass
Pushes up like a resurrected down-

Pour between the pebbles on the path.
Along the road, traffic punches holes
In the daylight, and beside the river,
The windmill runs hard, but not hard

Enough: the day is coming our way
Like holy chatter from the north.
High in the bankrupt, unbelieving
Hawthorns, a crimson rosella strikes

A note as pure as a boy soprano's
In chapel. Down the lane, the wattlebird's
Engine just will not turn over. A poem
Will sometimes do it for me.

Sometimes it only takes a word. Love
Returned like summer. Sunlight on a step.
There are days one can only endure.
And then there are mornings like this.

7. Saturday afternoon fever

It's Saturday afternoon a little after two, and my neighbour has started up his mower. The breeze is rising as I write, and it's coming from the east. We're close enough to the coast for that to insinuate showers, but right now the sun is staring down the clouds, which flap and dissemble like unconforming prayer flags and stream into the secular west. The sky is speaking my mind again. High in the elms, which are stripped bare and stretched taut against that sky, a currawong takes stock and takes it again, in case. A black and white moth prowls the pears hanging on the tree, and now some light rain falls like stardust. The swarthy grass shivers in the sunlight, and a mass of windfallen pears litters the ground like a poor man's booty. The exquisite voice of the grey butcherbird pipes its sweet and murderous phrases from somewhere other than where they're supposed to be, saying something quite other than what she means. And so it is that beauty entraps. Bowerbirds have been busy all day in the hedge working out what to do with themselves now that their time has come. Crimson Rosellas are keeping it surreal among the crabapples, and, above the drone of the mower, ravens have been practising their eccentric spelling.

8. *Overcast aubade*

There are days I wish
Would go on forever,
And this is one. And I
Wish I could spend
Its patient grey resources
Making everything as clear
As everything stood
In your eyes
When morning woke.

9. *Some very smart worlds on fire*
After we talked I walked into
The night and looked up. You
Never saw such a sky: what's left
Of the rest of everything
Grazing the black winter fields,
Pulling up time by the roots.

Transit of Venus

LAST NIGHT at eight, the Earth in its orbit
                    turned and threw its shadow—the aggregate
Of all our orphaned selves—over half the Orphic moon:
A sack dropped over the head of a god—Shiva, maybe,
Mugged by love, in the sacred glade of night.
And dawn today was a tungsten blaze
                          when I rose to poke my fingers in the fire's eyes:
The morning the fallout from the night before, a godly light turned way down
Low. And tomorrow night, Venus,
              who's been circling slantwise in her vestments
Since late May, has her second coming out, her first walk across the sun,
That fading star, since the century before last. We live in numinous days: the Earth
Stepping out of her own shadow,
                      love making a catwalk of the sun: so,
How could the city *not* be tossed about tonight like a salad in a cyclone?
Call it an East Coast Low, if you like: weather like this is the rough love
Planets make—those gods congealed, those tales of our olden days, our wilder
Ways—while we, like children, watch in fright from underneath eternity's bed.

What Happens if the Heart is Not Where the Home Is?

So, I'VE BEEN out of love with you
                        three years now. You weren't asking
   The right questions of me, I thought. *(And whose fault is that?)*
You weren't touching me often enough,
                             in enough of the right places. We fell silent with each other,
   And I swore I'd leave. It was probably the right thing
                                  to have done: my heart gone
On ahead; my soul sleeping rough on the well-made edges

   Of your bed. I lived three years an exile
                             in someone else's idea of home:
These understated hills (they roll, but they don't rock),
   These well-mannered paddocks, these gardens,
                             these quiet streets with their finishing-
School accents. But I stayed; I failed, really, to leave. I sat at my desk,
   Instead, and saved myself with metaphor.

My spirit estranged from where it dwelled; a dissenter
   In paradise; a marginal figure in the story
I was supposed to be living,
                     I made work I could not have made, happy.
   And metaphor proved me; I grew patient, slow; less obvious; *other*wise.
Until, against my will, I fell
                    from my tree and back in love again

  With the forest. Stop looking long enough
         and she'll find you where you were,
Wishing you were elsewhere, and nearly everything
  Were other than it can ever be. Bluewrens,
An old-fashioned sweetshop reincarnated, spill their gob-stopping voices
  All over my floor, and a ride-on
        trims the near distance.

And maybe it was unkind of me
       (if not unfair) to say that time that driving beneath
  The speed limit constituted for my fellow citizens the epitome
Of civic virtue. I take that—a certain distance—back.
          But I'll still be driving too fast,
  If that's okay (there are better laws to abide), only not too far away.
Home has waited me out. And here I am, and glad, on its threshold.
         If someone could just help me break the door down.

Break & Enter

THE COWSHED smells of apples
                     when I walk out of the wind.
   August is beside herself for miles around:
An arsonist without a match, a vandal loose
    In her own vacant house.
                      There's been a hole in one of the windows
Here since the start of summer, and through it now the end
    Of winter streams in.
But the scent is a slow thief's thank-you

Note. A rose—an artist
                 by any other name—has entered
   And broken out where summer broke on in. Camille Pissarro
Nods his perfumed head, a burglar
                         tired of taking, determined now to give
    Himself away. The flowerhead's
An impressionist explosion
               going off in pale increments
   At the end of a long green fuse;
                  it's a softly spoken argument

With a million points to prove;
                        a landscape admiring its own view
    Sideways through the glass. And in the room the stillness
Shifts and settles back, and the rose goes on,
    Rephrasing in fragrant, almost tranquil,
                            syllables the overwritten tropes
In which the world is out there telling
    A dozen different versions,
                    every moment, of the truth.

Something there is—an implacable sort
                        of surrender—that does not love
    The kind of wall a window makes between
What one sees and what one gets. At my desk
    I type and delete and type
                    and delete: I throw words at the glass
Aiming to crash the silence that keeps me,
                        to burgle my soul by degrees.
    Meanwhile, the cowshed smells of apples still,
                    and the wind plays an ill-tempered blues.

Old Beginnings

I WALK above the water
        at the edge of the woods,
  Where half the light is shadow, and half the shadow,
Light. Four cormorants fly from me; one white egret stays,
                safe in her past life on the far bank.
    Above the weir, they've poisoned half the hawthorns (so far) for not having been here
From the start; but what will the birds eat,
              still at home in their occupied territories,
    Until the old beginnings begin?

I sit on the bench above the water,
            my young dog at my feet, and wonder:
    Had I not picked up
            where you and I left off, where I was
Certain the beginning was done and the end was dusted,
    Where would I sit now and with whom?
                Would so much good have come?
Would sorrow have sanded me—pain handed me—back so hard?
    And well. One goes on. Bad decisions come good. Good things grow old;
                some die; some don't. Time starts to tell.

A life grows up around you
                        like a suburb. There used to be a shack
  In woods: now look! At fifty you turn, and there are rooms
All over the place down a very long hall; out the windows, street furniture,
    Cul-de-sacs, a dense geography. A whole lot of history.
                                    You'd have thought they'd need permission
Of some kind; you remember signing nothing. And you know you must be loyal
    To the life you seem to have. But it's hard:
                      there are other lives you might have led. Might yet.

Chiefly there is your given life, that other tongue,
                            crying out in its holy syntax, from somewhere
  Down the hall: the self they used to think of as one's soul;
The place, you know, before the woody weeds; the view
    Before the subdivision. And the bigger your life looks
                            the smaller it grows
Till your old self wants out; it wants *you* out. But here it sits companionably with you now,
  In the second person, at your desk, at the end of the day,
                        when the first child comes:

Can I do some drawings, Daddy?
                      And she takes your black ink
  And your blue, and the goose feather she found when you walked
In the paddocks yesterday, and she ransacks paper from your printer,
    And she draws herself a princess and she stains her small fingers and spots your floor
With her very near misses.
                    And the second child comes, asking
  If you know where he left his Lego catalogue.
                            And you never do and you don't again this time,
                      but you're glad

He's come, because he is fey and beautiful
    In a way that will always be misread, and life won't want to run
Any straighter for him
                            than it's run for you, and the best way to tell him that
    Is to hold him. And the third child comes,
And after he's sat drawing dinosaurs for ten minutes in your armchair,
    The dog arrives, too, and she tugs your jeans,
                            and then boy remembers:
                                  oh, yeah—mum said to come up for dinner.

It was always too late. The life you had
                      in mind was freer and fuller of time.
    But what did you know back then? The new beginning
You keep meaning to make is already well begun. It crowds
    Around you: every native and exotic species.
                                  It's not a way out
You need; it's a way more deeply in. Love
    Doesn't mean you to stop;
                  it doesn't want you to stint—
                            just to stay. To wait. Sometimes forever.

Birthday Letter #51

And no one suspects the days to be gods.
—Ralph Waldo Emerson

When we look into our own hearts and begin to discover what is confused and what is brilliant, what is bitter and what is sweet, it isn't just ourselves that we're discovering. We're discovering the universe.
—Pema Chodron

H<small>IGH</small> S<small>UMMER</small> one day;
      midwinter the next: the way it always went.
 The cosmos is bipolar, and the weather's always somewhere near
The edge. Each day is a god, you see, and the gods are in love,
            as gods always were,
 With fire and ice; and you don't believe in the gods, of course,
But each day they wake up believing
         in you again, and this one hangs around,
 Tough and profligate, all day
       and rains, in the end, all over the end
            of your fifty-first year on earth.

The world is a demented Buddha,
                    graven in your own image. She is a woman savaged
    On a city bus, a goddess defiled and thrown
                    like an obscenity into the suburbs; she is
Twenty children strafed in a classroom just shy of Christmas; she is
    A fire that steals a coastal town; she is two dollarbirds investing more
                    than they had to lose in the expansive light on the river; she is
Your own indomitable despair, your daughter's indefatigable delight.
                    The world, yes, is a world-weary Buddha, losing too much
    Sleep smiling kindly down on his own eternal intemperance
                                    across the vast trainwreck of time.

Rain falls near midnight, a casual act
                    of kindness. It walks the roof
    In stolen socks; it cracks compassion's code. Cold water carpet-bombs old
Asbestos ten unsteady feet above your head.
                    You begin forgiving the weather, you end up
    Forgetting yourself. Chaos goes on making love,
                    of course, with order; everything goes on dying
To be born. But you step out, almost forgiven, into the contrary world,
    Hoping again to do the kind of justice to your life
                    you'd want done on Earth,
                            and knowing now exactly where to start.

VI—Why You're *Here*

The Peach Blossoms on Station Street

Peach blossoms flare on Station Street: a rush
   Of love, a rage of remembering in August.

   I see them from the platform, where I wait in
Midwinter cold for my train. The blooms, unlike the train,

Seem to run early; each year it is the same.
   Do they know what they're doing? Aren't they

   Rushing into it? But beauty knows when. It's smarter
Than it looks, for wisdom grows lovely waiting.

And so, this flagrant open-heartedness, this almost
   Violent tenderness on Station Street, which runs

   To its own holiday timetable, and asks you out
Into the world—this is what you must make sure

You catch. There will be another train.
   Life is made of moments, and this is one,

   And each one takes about a lifetime to arrive.
Love, pretty in its season, takes courage—

The kind the peach trees, breathing the future out
   Beside the tracks here this morning, rehearse,

  Holding their breath, through three seasons at least,
Until the timing seems as bad as it could be. Wildness

Is the older order in us we keep forgetting to keep,
  And life is the love that form makes with time.

One Turning

Spring is in the peach trees   like morning in the library. And each
    Soft bloom flares an old truth   you get to grasp again. How many
More Septembers till you grow wise   as one turning of the earth?

Winter Comes In Overnight

Twilight, the sky is crystal clear.
The children dance with joy.
They shout and splash in the puddles.
—Chu'u Chu'ang I (tr. Kenneth Rexroth), "Evening in the Garden Clear After Rain"

I GO TO BED too late again, and in the morning,
            winter has come in. As if I've sleepwalked three
   Seasons round and woken in rags and tatters.
My heart is tired of working
   So hard to hope, but the world beyond
My window is a forest of voices, and the sky
               Is the colour of my children's eyes.

   And, for that matter, my own—
                in sadness and delight. A few clouds
Moving fast, halfway to heaven and meaning to rain,
   But this is a drought, and the day is soon done
With all thought of change. Wait, though, and it comes. Winter
     Concedes to spring. There is a joy in things, and it wants to break out,
               like the voices of children,
        like stars at twilight.

The Moon is Round and Fires Ring

THE MOON is round, and fires ring
                the city. Round as my third son's eye
  Is the moon tonight, but white where his is blue. From where I stand, out
On the deck in midnight air, and watch tomorrow sleep off today,
    The moon suggests a laser cut
                          in eternity's tent, a hole shot through the dark
Fabric of heaven.
          Where all the stars, paused in their burning, pour
  And pool and make light of all one ever had and lost.

Cicada Sonnet

Early afternoon feels like the morning
    Of the world, because you just woke it, love.

I look up from your email through a window five
    Trees hold open in the sunlight—maple,

Osage orange, elm, poplar, and oak—
    And it's like I'm a diver and this a sinkhole,

The sky the surface, blue with antiquity,
    Several storeys deep. Seven, eight

Dragonflies paddle the light, rowers in Eden;
    The scarlet tail-feather of a gang-gang sinks

Through the tide, and behind the beat of the monarch's flight,
    The bleat of a heron curses her luck in the dam.

And now cicadas shrill the underworld up
    From long ago, and this is your sonnet they sing.

Black Swan Moment

THE PROPOSITION was all swans were white,
    A thesis swans here never got to swim.

Like these two, slitting the silver scrim of morning
    Open to receive an early rain.

Each moment, if you find your way to it,
    Is unforeseen, improbable as this one—

Watched over by the only white thing here,
    The egret on the shore.
                          What makes the moment

Mythic is that the birds show up in it
    At all, inhabiting their black-swan cool

As if it were their everyday attire.
    Like you, imperfectly adapted, love,

To what the way of things requires. Your smile
    The white that flashes when the moment flies.

Comes a Time

THERE COMES a time in life when life won't come,
   Or won't come easy, when you call. Comes
A time enthralled by doubt as if all life were
    Drought.
               Comes a light rain now spilling like small change
From the pockets of the overcast, and a panic of grass
   Parrots across the fields, spreading like a rumour
Of rain in the hills.
              Who one was has wandered
   Far from home. And how can one begin to be again
When one *isn't* anymore?
              There is a fear as old as
   Geologic time that rises sometimes when one stands
A moment still; it wants to drown the laughter
   Of existence out.
              But that will never do.
                        The rain,
For one thing, is much too fine to die in, and anyway,
   Look, the birds are back, the fear that flew them
Passed, the grass their paradise again.

                    There comes
     A breeze and word of sunshine on the make. With
Each breath refute the fear, refuse to let your light
     Go out. With each breath begin again.
                              The moment
Is an empty lake, but it will fill with years, and time
     Will pass across its face like the hush that birthed
The earth, and your life will be again a place where children
     Play and stories start. Among them—only one among
Them—will be yours, too, made new, and wood ducks
     Will roost in your hair and loins and rain will fall
Like a sentence that doesn't mean to end and rivers
     Will rise and run in your veins and fire will start
In your heart.

               The hills around the city are old
     Like you and handsome and tired of summer
And they seem to welcome winter like a son. They
     Take his overcoat and hang it in the Argyle Apples,
They throw his weathered hat upon the fire
     And laugh. Stay, say the hills. Tell us all you've
Seen.
          In the midst of life you're asked to start again
     And don't know where—your life a book grown
Prodigal, biblical, improbable, a thicket in your mind,
     And the pen run dry and your hand arthritic. Write
It, then, this book, by waiting all its pages out. Write
     It, then, by driving home in failing light. Keep asking,
Though you know there won't be answers yet. Strange
     To think the man you'll be when you are well
Already wears this face, these clothes, this name,
     Already knows this book of yours by heart.

There comes a time when life arrives
Like dusk to the edge of the road. And if not
This dusk, then the next, your life will come. Like
The eagle to the ridge, like the winter to the hills,
Like the mind to the present moment and the future
To the past, your life will come and find you, friend,
And all your days will be illuminated pages, then,
From the book the world was writing for you
All along, and there will be no end to it, that life
You could not, for all your calling, find.
                                                The life
That will not seem to start is already well begun.

Dark Moon Sestets

THE MOON is dark all night, an absence
         day hardly knows how to wake from,
  And a frost sprawls the weary lawn. The high wind
That tore the night in two has fallen,
    And an easiness sets in. Yesterday the first rain
                in months; today, the first bud opens on the camellia,
The world's slowest ordnance going off like silence in soft rain.
    And the daffodils pick up their brief affair where they left it lie last September.

Where the ash in its pallor had installed
            panic at the bottom of the yard, it learns
  In the turning season to break out some tender moves
Again: kelp in sweet currents beneath
    The morning's tide. If you look
              the way I seem to recall a lover drinks you in,
You can see how the liquidambar lets summer's first green notes play,
    A composer's first fingerings in search of a chord.

The rain, this slim respite, is done
            by ten; the dry holds fast, and the watertable
  Knows it. But the tree draws up its dope
From way down deep, where the way things are outruns a drought
    That can't be chided to relent.
              But all things yield in time. Yesterday, too, other signs:
A daughter happy to bump against you conformably, as if you weren't a stranger,
    In the street, content to get about some frames of her Instagram
             life for an hour on your couch, your home her hearth a while.

The Last Day of September

T HE LAST DAY of September spent
                             alone with the light. It fell lascivious on the armchair
    By the window, and it tried to ask my sweater, draped there, out;
As if I were some shade that needed shifting,
    It steeped me, when I sat out its warmth a while
                             beneath the liquidambar,
Coming slowly into leaf; it gave the cat away as she lay lean in slender shadows
    In wait for prey she didn't have a prayer of taking;
                             and at the reservoir, where I walked late, it lacquered like slate

The surface of the lake and strained itself through
                             paperbarks and bracken to reach me on the track,
    As if it were a morning slept in way too late; as if it were a line,
It lured the blackfish up and reeled them in
    To breach like Southern Rights and let them flop
                             like catch too small to keep. Hope and grief all day, like tides,
Floated me from the anchor of each moment; all day long the light held.
    And when it left at last, it left the past it shaped all day alone
                             inside the memories it had cast.

Nine Pines on Kangaloon

For Deborah Bird Rose

A̲LL NINE PINES that line the street in pain
    Are transposed into a dark still fire,
Tonight, and the sooty owls and the parrots that roost
    The trees south of where I sit, carouse
Like gibbons in the hills, and the moon, almost
    At full term, has burned a smoke ring ten
Thousand light years round in the fabric
    God's best friend has pulled across the winter
Sky.
    There is a peace that's fallen on me,
    Much deeper than I or anyone has earned—
Except perhaps by holding out against
    Despair and working hard against the evidence
At hand, against the clock, reprising kindness
    In the face of cruelty and cant,
As steadily as these trees forgive the cold.
    The great work takes its first small steps
Inside the heart, and learns to turn the tides
    In time, but always harbours here.
                              The moon
Tonight's a pale hearth, a fire refusing,
    Though it gutters, to go out, and all
About, those who love us and all we loved
    On earth, and, half, too, of those our love
Disdained to reach, pitch their tents and light

    Their lamps and sit.
                      We keep among us, this once,
A quiet counsel, where all we never knew
    Is known and in no desperate need of being
Heard.
        Some wanted fire; you wanted the lighted
    Earth, and all the ages underneath
(And the fire there). I know tonight
    The calm that holds the river of your pilgrim
Tongue. I know from you, my friend, that living—
    Hard or hopeful, hollow or hallowed, holy
Or harrowed—must learn to block its ears to every
    Word that wants to hint at giving in.
This is the mercy moment, finally come;
    Tonight is all the justice you'd see done.

OF COURSE, it stops, all living, in the end—
    Just about the time you thought you'd got it
Down. But tonight, there is no end to all
    The goodness in the world, the life you've lived,
My friend.
          And all around the waxing moon
    The circle sits and says its prayers; the sky,
Which is a desert, hears them all, and down
    Among the planted pines, on Kangaloon,
The answers play in pictographs and signs,
    In languages, in which these more than merely
Human tongues want us to know our human
    Lives are given so that all that is not
Just one human life can be the world
    It is, with or without us—asking of us,
While we stay, only our songs, our care.

    AND PERHAPS the joy we knew will never come
Again—although, this frog-pocked night, when all
    The rain we waited for all year and then
Began to think today would never end,
    Ends; this night when all feeling stills,
This early night in June begins to feel
    A little like the last day of school
Felt to the child one was and now one's children
    Are. And perhaps the pain will clear like rain;
Or perhaps it never will, but one will learn
    A deeper thing than joy, a farther reach
Than joy can teach, a love like that the earth
    Extends to all that happens, and all that ceases,
On it.
        There is a stillness now the trees
    Instruct by standing every thought upon
Its head. A peace that waited fifty years
    For you to make it, or know it, rather, like
A friend, who's stood here with you all along:
    Your Self.
           Which is all our selves, the swamp, the dragon-
Fly, the dead, the river that bears us on;
    Tonight's a weathered balm that understands
Calamity and how to break it like
    A human heart and mend.
                One needs to learn
Lament the way the grasses won't relent,
    But rise where all else falls, and fail, themselves,
In fallow times, in flood, in fire and drought—
    But, after, draw another breath and start
The past again and call the future back

From where it lost its faith.
                              One needs to pine
Like pain reprised in kind, to mourn like dawn,
    The way each day reboots the whole relentless
Thing again—forgiving past days for passing,
    Oneself for forgetting one's Self, for passing through
The fallen things with less respect, remorse,
    Than they deserved, less witness than they'd earned.
One needs to rest in all one's loss, to make
    One's living a getting on in fellowship—
Like this line of pines on Kangaloon—
    Against the meagerness that wastes the earth.

AND IN THE MOONLIGHT, as if to prove the point,
    The rake leans against this other tree,
A liquidambar, which has let the last year,
    And all the years before, it seems, fall,
And stands, content with all the work it left
    Undone all day upon the winter lawn,
The lazy battalions of leaves, arraigned the way
    The weather, blowing June in from the west,
Has laid them out, forgetting for now the battle
    They thought they'd come to fight, becoming, instead,
Landscape again, ground replete with every
    Lore, except the rules of war: a scattered
Camp, embers unraked, a coming season.

All the Campbelltowns

For Daniel & for Michelle Rickerby

PLACE TAKES TIME to fathom, and they've ploughed
    The many Campbelltowns under and tarred them over

That there were before this Blaxland Road I walk
This season of the geebungs and the car yards, of wild

Honey and bluewren. If I knew *here* as here knew
    Me, I'd read in flowerings of petrophile the running

    Of Macquarie Perch, which used to swim a name
In which Dharawal rivers ran.
                          But place takes time

To hear, congeals in eras, finds a local dwelling,
    A family of phrase one needs long years to over-

    Hear. Belonging is a practice and place will school
You in it once you start to shed your skin. But I've

Been caught too long, since landing here, in knotted
    Nets of memory to forget.
                          To let the Wollondilly

    Delve me like a gorge. Yet all the Campbelltowns
There are and were—the one before the singing, the one

That sang, the farm that fleeced the forests and fattened lambs
    And counted sheep—were immanent beneath my feet

    And wanting to drum their many names and hum their fame
In every dieselled breath I drew.
                        Time takes place

In places—takes us with it, if we will. But time
    Takes time to rhyme the diviner to the divine.

    Meantime the Picton hills are shrill with grief too still
And joy too long deferred for my slow words to feel.

Poems take time to take place, and this one, wanting time
    And keening place, remains unready to be read.

    So let it, like a place, improvise itself and riff
On lines inherent in what the present inherits

From times gone past and be the ears that overhear
    What's coming in all that has already been overcome.

The Schoolhouse

                I<small>N THE SCRUB</small>
                    That runs the schoolhouse round—
                            The second growth yellow box,
              The ribbon gum, the geebung, the bracken
And the oak—all afternoon from every broken compass point,
        The miners, in voices like the peels and plaints
                Of every child
                        Who sat inside this weather-
Board box in every one of 1500 families
Of weather, and wished the day and all the lessons
      They had no idea that one day they might wish
                  They'd learned would end the moment
They sat down—all day, in fact, at six beats to the bar,
         From every timbered and forgotten point
                Of view, without a hope
                    Of schooling time
To race, but keeping at it anyway, the miners ring the bell that stops the day
         And wanders all its indoor lessons
                Out, and walks them down across the gorge
                      And through this light that talks
                              In tongues and slicks with fall
            The leaves that throng the end of summer,
                And walks a hundred happy
Dairy farmers' sons and gardeners' girls, paroled,
                    Through every year that's happened since,
              Through butcherbird blues and wattlebird rap, more or less
                    Safely home.

The Teacher

For Roderick Kefford

    THE BEST teacher I knew taught me what I love
        By loving it himself; he trailed it like a gown around
                The school and into class behind him, where it fell
        Like light conversation among us: but, in fact, it was
A world. It was the whole library at Alexandria
        He carried, and it stooped him, like a poacher's sack
                Of hieroglyphs, and he taught it by heart, that old canon,
        As if he had begun where that library stopped. He opened
A library in me, the teacher; he began a better fire.
        He was a cursive script escaped in an antique hand,
                A sentence that ran wild and elegant in a taciturn land,
        And what he loved is what language says before it means
And how it keeps eternity awake long after. From how
        He went, I learned the news: poetry divines the world.

He walked in iambic pentameter. His feet were dactyls—
    Anapests on Tuesdays. School was an emergency he sped
        Through, leaning us all into our futures. For there was
    Never any other time than now, and there was no better
Place than this. *The readiness was always all; the play always*
    The thing. And something mattered only language led to:
        Each sentence a piece of the cosmic string that everything
    And all of us are sung on. He opened books, and divinities
Leaped out, distances; your whole life leaped out, one life
    Among so many, any old heaven, but entirely your own.
        He was like us—*a schoolboy, a lover, a (tin) soldier*—only older;
    For he was Mr Bennet, too. He was Orwell. He was Prufrock.
It wasn't hard to picture him reading Eliot before Eliot
    Discovered cats. He came in old, you sensed, and spent

A lifetime, learning—by teaching us, line after line, metaphor
    By metaphor—the godlike trick of growing younger than
        The world. The books he opened kept on opening;
    They keep on opening still. They let the world out; they
Let us back into the secret of who we are: each of us,
    The other, if you reach down far enough. The lessons
        The best teacher teaches—less by saying than by being
    What she means, or he—stay taught. With his whole life,
As much of it as he can catch, he teaches you your own, long
    Before you're ready, so that, when, at last, you are,
        You'll know how to walk it like a forest and how to speak
    It like a library and how to care for it as if it were on loan.

A Memory of Fall

Spring is a memory of fall.
—Jocelyn Fraser

T HIS SPRING MORNING
                        feels like an afternoon
    Winter forgot to spend: clouds torn
From an old Manchester catalogue,
                    the season stalled in the trees. The wind pretends

To blow; the rain holds out
                    promises you know it will not keep. In truth,
    It's not *that* cold; it just feels like it wants to be. But look now: sunlight
Spills from midday's seams and runs the barefoot grasses,
                    laughing, the way you used to laugh,
                            when grief was still a child.

Spring

For John Edmonds & for Alan Holley

1.

Birdsong is the friendliness
                    of nature, the way the world forgives.
  This September morning, down which four days
Of rain peter and pour again, the antiphonal song of magpie larks—
              half statement of claim, half drunk love song
  To a sober god—is how the lyric comes. And pulls you from the wreck of night.
Even beauty does violence sometimes,
                        and things that shouldn't,
  Fray. Life rends. But the phrases the birds exchange
                  befriend all brokenness and shut all distance

2.
Down. Music—some said, some sung,
                some acted out—is the language
  Of the internet of things. In times when most of what is real transpires
In pixels and days pass by in digits, when half the world can be
  Your friend but never know the shape of you,
                        the grace note of your evening voice,
Friendship is a revolutionary act. Life depends on how we differ;
  Our wealth is how we take delight in that.
                And kindness is the highest human art.

3.
My glory, said a poet once,
                              is that I had such friends. Friendship, then,
    The art of giving something like a damn, is the poetry of wings. Disabled by living,
We're enabled again by the antiphonal grace of the friend,
    A beauty that answers sorrow, a truth that answers lies.
                                        The limbs of the pear tree, trimmed in winter,
Leaf out now, like soft apologies for the rain, and the peewees pass triadic figures
    Hand to hand across the keys, fingerings
                                    that ask the first white blooms to break.

The Iris

For Heather Tredinnick, my mother, at Eighty-five, 2 February 2022

N OT SO MUCH the white iris
                        in the garden, dishevelled
              after rain, but the blue—furled
  Inside its dignity, hat on straight, a small choir of them bunched here, as it
Happens, on the bench. Amethysts of the organic world
    (And her birthstone, as I recall). Along the creek, cherry trees make ready,
Through ten warm years each year,
                to blossom, if they're lucky, for a week.

But what passes, it transpires, is the only
                            thing that lasts—the anguish
              of the child, the ease of middle years, the high
  Notes, the few best days—and waiting makes all loveliness over into its own.
When it comes to birds, I couldn't say, but I find her in the hedges
    With the wrens; I hear her in the piping
                        of the blackbird in the dusk. Trumpets
In the flue pipes, pigeons at the pedals;
                  fanfares and ligatures and runs: Each human life's a fugue

Too hard for anyone to play
      half as well as anyone might like—
   given the instrument, given the time.
 Some parts of it are going to have to wait. But the world, in truth,
Is made of music, begun again by every lyric act—a mother's
 Moves so many among them—
        and devotion is the divination of the real.
Your days a sacred music, then, and a pastoral air or two.
    A phosphorescence, like a happy cipher, that goes on.

Holding My Father's Heart

For my father on his Ninetieth Birthday, 7 October 2021
After Joshua Yeldham, "Holding My Father's Heart"

IF I COULD hold my father's heart,
    My hand would be a garden bed,
And all the years he's turned, the art

He's practised on the plants, might shed—
    Like leaves, or evening light—some truth
More true than most of what's been said:

On how to live a life of use,
    On how to raise a choir up,
Without much of a voice to use

Yourself. My hand would be a cup
    In which the seasons pooled and rang
And dogs and children's names ran up

And down suburban halls and sang
    The modest lessons thrift had schooled
My father in—the soil's slang

For prospering on care and rules
    That tend to work no matter what
The fashion says, for older tools

Are more the kind of thing that God
    Had by, when first he dreamed the Garden.
How light are ninety years to hold.

The world when you were young fell hard
    From war into depression. You came
Into a world in spring, time's gardens

Beginning again, a curate's time,
    The season of the shepherd. The world
Was a parish, the world was a dairy farm,

When you took your first steps in it. The Word
    Was God, and the word was God was good
With a spade. And not too bad with numbers—

He saved more than he spent, they said;
    And you learned to see a berry where others
Saw only straw. You understood,

Inside the hope that raised you, that faith
    Without delight or doubt is a plant
Without a prospect. And from your father

You learned to take the kind of chance
    Creation takes with time—small moves
Achieve the greatest ground. And patience,

The art of the Earth, will always prove
    The wiser way in the end. If I
Could hold my father's heart, this trove

Of moments, small ways standing by,
    It wouldn't be a weight of words
I held, but a kind of levity,
A lightness of touch, a flight of birds.

Arms & A Boy

For Daniel

That is what I have
to give you, child, stories,
songs, loquat seeds,

curiously shaped; they
are the frailest stay
against our fears…
—Robert Hass, "Songs to Survive the Summer"

M̲Y SON, I want to tell you
    This: we belong to each
Other, as we belong

To no one else. I am yours,
    Your father for all time.
You are not mine

In the same way, for you,
    Like all children, belong
To your own life. But

You were given to me
    To care for and to deliver
Into the years that wait

For you, the story
    That will write you,
The lyric of your days.

But among all the work
    I have to get done,
At the heart of the love

I am here on earth
    To practise, you are,
My boy, and your brothers

And your sisters. My
    Work is to have you
Know your beauty

And to help you find
    Your way out into
Everything that wants

To love you, child,
    And be loved by you
In return. My work

Is to have you know
    How beloved you are
On the earth. Do you

Know that my heart
    Is a house where you
Are always welcome?

Do you know that my life
    Means a large part of any-
Thing it means because

You are my boy, and I am
    Your father? But our
Belonging is freedom, Dan.

It is made of beginnings.
    I lay no claims on you.
Your life is your own to keep

From me. And though I'll fight
    Forever to have you near
And to have you know

My love, I wouldn't want you
    Ever to know me or love me
Because someone says you must.

There is a place in my love
    For all the sorrow I feel
Without you, my boy.

You live in my house,
    In my blood, my words;
You live in my silence

And in my days. All my days
    And my nights, though
I may never share them

With you, though you may not
    Want to say my name, you rest
And you riot in my house.

I see you, you see, no matter
    How much you think you do not
Want to see me. I want you

To know this: you have
    The best love a boy could
Hope for, and you have it all

Your life: a father's arms,
    A father's life, which he
Would surrender for you

No matter how little
    You think you want that
Or him. You will need

A father's love one day more
    Than you know you need it
Now. And you will have it.

You have it now. It's hard
    From a distance to know you
Know that, but I believe

You do. And feeling that
    Is enough to feel
From you in return.

Once, when you were stormy
    And very young,
I nursed you and lullabied

You. Once, I watched you
    Walk. I knew every name
You spoke for things, and

I loved every name you made
    For me, the father you loved
With the ferocity you love

Or hate all that life offers
    You. We read. I showed
You gods. I taught you

How to hold a bat and how
    To bend a ball and address
A woman. You made me feel more

Worthy of my life than any-
    One will ever do again.
I love you now in silence

Mostly, and in distance
    And in dreams. My love
Is stronger than my hope

And stronger yet than my
    Despair. I will hold you
Again, but even if I never

Do, I will love you and
    My heart will be your home,
And I live my life, I write,

I teach, I love others,
    I love birds I taught
You to hear and see and love,

I live my life in welcome
    For you, and my sadness
Without you is glad, too,

That you are in the world
    And that you are my son.
All I can give you is my

Self. And I give it,
    And I hope it finds you,
And I give it without hope.

And giving it, I feel forgiven
    A little, for losing you; I feel less
Lost, more at home again,

Though far from you,
    In that other home
We share: the common-

Place commonwealth
    Of all that breathes. I give
You nightjars and fruit-

Bats; I give you blue
    Wrens and books, my son,
And words in which worlds

Wander and sing. I give you
    Gratitude, mine for you,
And yours, I hope, for

All things: your own life,
    Your gifts, the love others bear
You. And I hope when you

Get to hear of it, you will
    Know one day that all along
You had the shelter

Of this love, a dauntless,
    Frail stay against all
Fears. A world in which

You were loved beyond
    Counting, beyond reason,
For being just exactly
    Who you are.

The Nature of All Things

1.

CHANGE IS IN the nature of all things:
    Some change comes soft; some hard. A child
Learns to talk in grammatical increments
    And to walk in an afternoon. A marriage
Lasts a decade, two hearts shift, it bends
    Or it ends. One day you're twenty-six,
The next you're fifty-four.
                          The trick is not to hope
    To slow time down, or to wish the end
Away; the trick may be to find the pattern
    In the passing, and fall in with it, the beat
Of the eternal inside the racing heart of every
    Shifting thing. Climate, that house that is
Our only home, is change, itself. Wanting
    Too much, addicted to ourselves, we've dosed
It up on speed, and who knows where it's likely
    To be next.

2.

              THE WORLD our children enter
Will cause more grief than the one we found.
    Climate change moves cities, shifts plates: in thirty
Years, Melbourne will be Adelaide; Bendigo,
    Alice Springs. The weather—whose mind
Was never less made up than now—asks us
    To make ready for whatever it decides to be.
A garden is a school where they teach you
    How to learn. How to see, to be.
                                  A garden
Is the future planted in the past; change is most
    Of what a garden grows. Never still, never
Done, it thrives, if it thrives, by learning how
    To live with what it's got. Among plants you learn
Not how things will turn out, but the grace to let
    Them come.

3.
              A GARDEN IS a changing room—
A nursery where patience bites its nails and
    Bides our time and grows its hair and lets
Its becoming come. And invites us to our
    Own. A garden will teach you how to wait:
In love, if not in hope. Here you can learn
    Readiness, restraint, resilience—reconciliation
With the way things want to be. A garden
    Is a masterclass in flux, a short-course in fore-
Sight, a masterplan in chance.
                            In this one poles
    Meet: North lives side by side with south; east
With west. None of what came from those
    Far places saw this coming, but here they are,
Learning each other's children's names and
    Letting their best guess at the future come
And making plans to keep each other real.
    A garden is the future planted in the past,
A forest growing into a single mind. A mind
    Learning how to change—and how to teach
Ours how to change. A way finding itself
    By staying put and straying ever closer
To where it always was.

The Gardens of Beijing

For Huang Shaozheng (Hunter) & for Jidi Majia & for Jodie Williams

1. A Hundred Flowers

Assembled here, like silence anxious to be sound,
 The trees in Lu Xun's yard come into leaf. Beside

The library, eleven take the field, and stand, surprised
 To find these jumpers on their backs—a season's brand

New strip. They line up 4–4–2, their shadows fallen
 At their feet, the moves they won't remember later

How to make. The plane trees wear their camouflage
 Fatigues—white poplars barracked very close to home.

They bring to mind the boy we walked past yesterday,
 My love, a soldier marching Beijing Jie, and bearing

Unexploded ordnance, a tray of Singapore Orchids,
 A box of spring, cerise and white in Beijing grey

The softest fusillade you never heard explode,
 A garden on parade, not quite one hundred flowers

Blooming in a soldier's arms beside Tiananmen
 Square. And every half-embarrassed step he took

Rang out into the crowd at dusk, *I don't remember
    Signing up for this.* They bring—the trees, this boy—

To mind, my son, back home; their thinking greens a little
    More each day; they carry last year's fruit like bombs

They're dreaming up the nerve to throw. Do these
    Magnolias—their fashion-conscious dirty pink,

Their classic cream—remember how they grew inside
    My childhood days? My girl would climb the plum trees first,

My other son would be the nesting jays. But it's
    The lilac weed the garden hands have left to flower

In frost-burned lawn that speak to me: With luck, that's how
    I age, and fail. And everywhere one walks on earth

A life has stopped, a life's begun: the tender fall
    Of light at noon among us here remembers this.

It takes a life to make a moment last; it takes
    A world of time to grow a garden steep with light.

2. The Belly of Things

WE WENT TO THE GARDEN to look down on the city,
    And there it was beneath us, all the power men

And women believe they wield, none of it of much
    Consequence in time—all the beauty, the distortions

Of the truth, the lovely lies, the yellow tiles,
    The eunuchs and the concubines, the bound feet,

The wisdom and the reverence, the cruelty, the cant,
    The rhyme—and all of it beside us now.

We stood where art should stand: outside, near-
    By, apart.
            And from there, all that's always forbidden

Was a tangerine abstraction now: the wall
    A grey chimera now, a low horizon halfway down

The sky, the whole arrangement abstracted further
    By the smog of spring, and below, a daub of green,

The stubborn brightness dark in the belly of things.

    ~

    But before this, we had walked into peonies.

And much to our surprise. The lower ground,
    Just inside the east gate in the middle afternoon,

A rococo riot of tincture and form, an elegant
    Dissent. And beyond that, tulips, platoons pulled

Taut across the foothills, their bands of colour—
    Vermilion, magenta, cream—a fragrant Rothko,

Form decanted to tone, each tint a season
    Of mind transfigured and reconciled, side by side,

And spread across this world of tone distilled,
    A sheen of post-industrial silt, washed in on winds

From the mountains of the south, and brushed
    Like distemper across everything.

~

                The path
That gave us the city led us back to the peonies
    Through pines, which stood, in their parade-

Ground fatigues, as still as time would like to
    Like to learn to stand. And I beside her.

3. When I was Young

THE FARTHER FROM HOME I stray the closer I come
    To my self. Or is it that far from familiar selves,

We find a home we had not known we'd lost—
    The rest of our belonging, the tents, the flags,

The photos? The tulips in the parks are gypsies.
    They've travelled worlds to make this camp.
                                      One's self

A diaspora, too, one sees now—scattered before you
    Began. And most of who we are is other than

We are, and here, where one had never been
    And scarcely knew a word, one found oneself

In kin. So much of what one always meant
    One finds out in translation; and friendships old

As time one forges at first glance.
                            Outside
    The café where I sit, the old folks take

The long march slow, and swing their arms and speak
    Of growing old, beneath the gingko limbs,

Which green and grow young.
                        In here, a song
    I know but cannot name starts up, an ease

Earned hard and spoken sweet on nimble keys.
    I have to ask the girl who waits on us what song

This is I've always loved. She checks and writes
    A Zen garden in two scripts, on my napkin:

"Peace Piece." The ostinato in the bass
    Is the Beijing afternoon, its treble these bulbuls

Here, grace notes in grey light. On Shilipu,
    Another horn goes off—the right note in

The wrong score.
               Another magpie tacks
    The garden's length, trailing the summer behind,

And the noisome canal looks pretty in the sun.
    In flight, I think, the bird could be a paper

Plane I made by hand and launched as if
    It were my life, way back when I was young.

The Love Song of the Forest & The Field

...and gives to airy nothing
a local habitation and a name...
—William Shakespeare, "A Midsummer Night's Dream"

                          Y OU ARE the dance
                        I prayed for, love; I am the prayer
                That danced you free. I am the supper
           You earned, Beloved, dancing
                      All of time stock still. You are
      The forest in my blood and the wildness
                In my woods, my leaves. And *I?*
       I am whatever it takes to make
                      Your grove my groove; I am the blue
In your distances; the stranger in your trees and
             The water in your well; I am
                            The list inside your
             Listening. And,
                     Kissing,

                    We steal each other's
               Silver voice and with them smith a single
        Stream, the silence that's been running
                          Under all our selves, and all along.
                               I am the fire in your grate,
             My love, and you are the warmth
                  I make there.
                     We are the very house,
            In fact, of love, and tonight we are
                          Its only guests, and we are the drunken
        Ground it burns to, all around the sober edges
                  Of our delight.
                        I am the wilderness
                    In your underworld. Where I cried
                     And cried

                       Not knowing your name,
                But knowing you would come. You are
           Every broken step I take there now,
                        Inside the old growth of our original
                                   Freedom. You're the water
                In my well, the birds in my bath;
                     You're the butcher
                 And the baker and the fingers in my till;
                And *I*? I am the curses on your
                                 Tongue, the holes in your pocket,
           The birds on your unruly conference call; and your lips
                  Are a thirst that all the rivers
                       In all the worlds
                             Will never quench.

311

                    Oh, I kiss the pieces
                Of you whole, she says; the whole
            Of you to pieces. I fall apart
                    In you, he says, and apart from you
                                I am nowhere and I am no one;
            Except that in all the world, I am all
                        The words
                That say you best. I am the sleep
                                That dreams you up and drinks you
            Down again, and I am the body that runs
                    Off with your lawless soul.
                                I am the sentence you serve,
                        And I am every one
                    Of your terrible crimes
                                Against banality.

I Am My Beloved's, & My Beloved is Mine

For Rohan and Mariza

E̲ACH AFTERNOON two black
   Ducks land in the grass and lodge
By the water-trough through the dusk.

   The silence between them
Is deep and it's most of what they share
   And they would be nowhere else
And with nobody else, and there is
   Something beyond hope, and this
Is how it looks, fallen on the lowly
   Grass, she the rose of Sharon, he
The apple among the trees
   Of the wood. And from my shelf,
The clock repeats its old lie, and
   He drinks and flares the green
In his wings and says rise up,
   My love, and come away. Or
Something like that. For, lo, she
   Replies, the winter is past, the rain
Is over and gone; the time of the singing
   Of birds is come. And they rise
And eat from the seed of the hens
   And return and lie down in each
Other's delight until night
   Finds them out and he says:

Come, my beloved, let us go
    Forth into the field, or something
Like that, and they do.

    There are seven virtues,
At least, and some of them are small
    As bluewrens, and some as great
As silver poplars, but none matters
    Beside, and none counts without,
What visits us beyond reason and
    Outstays its season and makes the world
A garden again. And two birds.

    Love is strong as death,
I think, watching them articulate
    Eternity in their flight.

Imagine an Afternoon

IMAGINE an afternoon,
Then, in early May. Light
Rain since dawn, and the day tops out at seven,
Maybe eight, degrees. In the high country, the first snows. Winter
In the offing. Heavy
As borrowed coin
In autumn's back pocket.
On dusk, the wind gets up
And the light sallows, making of the last moments
Of daylight
A sepulchre,
In which you can smell the middle
Of the year, the waiting days, walking your way
Like prophets. Fragrant with time, high
Deserts, old riffs and plaints.
There will not be a day colder than this
All year, no matter what the locals say.
And nothing, I notice, can ever keep the landscape
Out (of my life) or hold my longing in,
No matter where I am
Or how I turn
My back on every holy thing
But you.

Why You're Here;
In Case One Day You Need to Know

1.
D<small>ON'T OUTSOURCE</small> your Self. You *are*
What you're here for. You are where
You need to go and why and how. And
You are the company you need to keep.
You are the way you need to wander
And you are the place you need
To make, and not just for yourself.

2.
      TO COME TRUE IS WHY
They sent you; to see off your fears;
To outsmart all you keep thinking
You know; to grow clever as a tree,
Holy as the bluest light, old as rivers,
Useful as a stone temple in the soft-
Spoken mouth of a valley ten thousand
Feet up in the highest range of hills
Earth knows how to find. You are
Here to find out why you're here—
Just you, just now—and why you've
Been given just these hands and only
So much to hold onto. You're here
To fall back all the way, if you can,
Into the beauty you arrived with, the
Beauty you cannot quite convince
Yourself you carry, for the world
Is often ugly when you look there
For yourself. And you're here to die
Back out of others' bad ideas of who
You are and what they reckon you're
Worth.

3.
      YOU'RE HERE TO LEARN
To walk the way that only your feet can
Teach you. You're here to find a way
To reach in and draw from the wound
That weeps you the sting that sings
The hymn of how you alone can heal
A small piece of world, beginning where
You are, the way it hardly knew it
Wanted healing. You're here to work
Out how to dwell in your life, at last,
The way the note the bell will strike wells
In the bell. How it waits. How it rings.

4.
      YOU'RE HERE TO DIVINE
The world a bit, to walk the god in you
Out with you, to make your moment
On earth worthy of the suffering it costs
You. And those you love. And the earth.
You're here to keep coming undone, to
Keep opening, like an answer toward its
Question, like sound toward silence, like
An echo toward a voice, like one toward
Another. Like water, you're here to run.
You're here to throw the light that only
You can throw. Like a shaft. Like
A blanket. Like a party.

Drop Anchor

Drop your anchor in the current hour:
   Make harbour in the present tense. Find

   Your stillness in the turning tide. Make
Of your sorrow a boat and float ashore.

   No other time than this; no other place
Than here; no one else but you. The pain

You feel is only what it costs to be. Your
   Stillness is the neap between the tides.

Epilogue

Page One

For Jodie Williams

THE MORNING was hail; the afternoon smoke; the dusk
   An Antarctic bluster, a sleeper's wake.
                                     Midnight, after the frenzy had played out,
Struck its single dark note, high in the register, and held it till dawn.
   In the wetlands, rank with sedge,
                               the water has retreated to a pool
The morning's downpour hardly touched, but it's enough
   For the snipe, who's returned from summer tundra farther
North. All she knows are intimacy and distance and where
   To put them down.
                       I watch her this morning assay her shore, and
With the scatter of her rapid feet make a jazz bar of a drought.
   Hers, the small, fast steps we need to learn to take—in the face
Of all that burns and fails so fast.
                         She gives one hope, the shore-
Bird, forgiving in the wealth of her solitude the poverty of our welcome,
   Landing back inside her self.
                           And you at the piano, all
The broken mornings, love, wake in me the same hope, each note
   A pipi plucked from mud.
                          Your fingers have not forgotten, through decades
Of disuse, the demi-semi-quavers they ran when they were young,
   But forty years have taught you how to feel what music costs.
Leaning into the keyboard like the snipe into her shore,
   You reprise an older summer you fly south: the rain that refrains

The mirror in the mirror, the lament. Page one of each a corner
    You're not ready yet to turn.
                                    Your fingers falling all around
The heart of every beat, you conjure the stars you fly by
    And let them loose inside the house, each a piece
Of an antique peace I caught the shattered edge of late last night.

Notes

Notes

"Standing", p. 31
To stand in the light of the world: I have in mind the actual light falling that afternoon on the rough-barked apples, and all about the shores of Erowal (the St George's Basin), but you might hear an echo in my phrase of some usages in *John*, where "light" is a motif. For instance, *John* 8:12—"I am the light of the world" and *John* 1:5—"And the light shineth in darkness; and the darkness comprehended it not." The poem also considers the idea of the standing of trees—the legal rights of other beings than humans.

"An Old Lament", p. 35
A small elegy in the form of a sijo, for a friend taken too soon. And a lament many have made—why do the scoundrels prosper while the angels fall. The sijo is a Korean form, of which there are a number in this book. Among many other secular and sacred constraints that attend the form, and which I hope I have honoured, each of the three lines of a sijo is meant to be fourteen to sixteen sound units long (I've interpreted that as fifteen syllables). This one is set in Bowral, Gundungurra Country, along Mittagong Creek.

"Several Birds & A Dog", p. 36
A sijo pair: my own improvisation on the sijo form. This one is set at the Cecil Hoskins Reservoir on the Wingecarribee.

"Before the Day", p. 37
This poem, written in Sanctuary Point (Erowal; Dharawal Country) on the South Coast of New South Wales, alludes to the Chinese poet Qu Yuan, to whom the birth of lyric poetry is attributed in China; to a river along which he wrote and died, the Miluo (340–278BC), where I was a guest at an international poetry festival in 2019.
My river is small: Tomerong, and not mine except in imagination and love.
Another poet says: Gregory Orr in many poems in *Concerning the Book that is the Body of the Beloved*, such as these lines: "Catastrophe? It's just waiting to happen./ Loss? You can be certain of it."

"Invoice", p. 42
This poem was written in the Lu Xun Academy in Beijing, part of a conversation with Bulgarian novelist Zdravka Evtimova, a guest with me on the academy's international residency program in April 2019.

"The Lyrebird", p. 45
I wrote this poem as one of many sestets on a Bundanon residency in 2010. Most of the poems I wrote there became "The Wombat Vedas." This sestet always felt different from the others; although I published it in pamphlets and anthologies, I kept it for this collection because of its themes—the nature of creativity, the practice of beginning where you are with what you've got. It's dedicated to Debbie Lim because I wrote it in correspondence with her about Chinese poems. I was working that stay on a book about the weather, to which the first two lines allude. The lyrebird encounter happened when I took a drive. The boobook sang most nights the only song it knows—its name.

"Whitefaced Heron on the Bong Bong Flats", p. 47
The Bong Bong flats, or "commons," are a tongue of floodplain along the Wingecarribee, a burial site for the Gundungurra, where European settlers first attempted to settle. Until the first flood washed them higher up hill. When this poem was written (and "Walking Easter Sunday Down), I used to often walk, with my young family, a track that runs along the river there. Whitefaced herons frequent the place.

"The Artist & His Model", p. 48
The poem makes a response, almost ekphrastic, to Matisse's "The Artist and His Model." It invokes the imagery of the coastline of Northern New South Wales, where I wrote it.

"I'd Like to Write a Poem", p. 50
This poem arose from frustration and sadness at not having written a poem in a while and noticing how much the dusk and the tones playing in my heart just then seemed to warrant a response in words. Writing, "I'd like to write a poem…" I began. As one does. (I may have had in the back of my mind the title of William Carlos Williams's *I Wanted to Write a Poem: The Autobiography of the Works of a Poet*, New York, New Directions, 1977. Williams is a favourite poet,

a surprising influence on my work. I have named a dog in his honour.

"The News (Poetry Tells)", p. 51
This poem responds to William Carlos Williams's famous assertion, quoted as my epigraph.
Under the breath of the god: I have in mind Hildegard of Bingen. A CD of her songs is called, after one of her meditations, *A Feather on the Breath of God*.
Where the money has never stopped/Changing hands: Jesus and the money lenders in the temple: a story told in, I think, all four gospels. And I have carried all my life an image of the beauty and inappropriateness of the "collection" or offertory, taken up in my childhood church by elders in special small carpet bags and counted by my father and others in the back rooms after the service.

"A Beginner's Guide to Wabi-Sabi", p. 57
A poem written after an afternoon on one of the beaches north of Wollongong, New South Wales—Austinmer, I think. The title and the organising idea play with the Japanese philosophy of *wabi-sabi*, which I take to assert the beauty of transience and imperfection; the loveliness of falling short and irregularity. And a home-made quality that attends beautiful and authentic lives and works of art.
The surf choppy and irascible: a line ("the camels galled, sore-footed, refractory") from T S Eliot's "The Journey of the Magi" plays in the background of my phrasing.
If beauty is truth: Keats's "Ode to a Grecian Urn": "Beauty is Truth, Truth Beauty—That is all/ Ye know on earth, and all ye need to know."
No one's telling it straight: Emily Dickinson: "Tell all the truth but tell it slant", Poem 1263.

"The Book of Daniel", p. 60
A Christening sonnet for my son. It includes references to the story of Daniel in the Christian *Bible*.

"The Sword & The Pen", p. 61
A poem, for the same son, which records a small domestic moment, when Daniel was perhaps five. The poem plays with the old adage that the pen is mightier than the sword.

"Dog Sonnet", p. 63
The family dog "Honey" was, as you'll guess, a collie.
The TV series every child watched in black and white: "Lassie".
The world was not yet too much for us: this alludes to Robert Frost's poem "Directive": "Back out of all this now too much for us,/ Back in a time made simple by the loss/ Of detail…"

"After a Long Drought", p. 64
The particular lake I have in mind here is Weereewa (Lake George) near Collector in New South Wales. The lake is endorheic, having no streams feeding it or flowing from it. It may be over a million years old—the oldest living inland lake in the world—and it once flowed into the Yass River, till the Cullarin Range rose and cut it off. It has in other words lived many lives already, and most of the time it retreats under the surface.

"Sometimes, A Shallow Sea", p. 65
See previous note. This Weereewa poem is a Sijo. My friend and mentee, Kate Lines, drives past the lake most days to work, and has kept a close and loving watch on her for years.

"Telling It Slant", p. 66
The title of this sestet, a small domestic lyric, considers how meaning is made, the role of metaphor in that; it plays with Emily Dickinson's line: "Tell all the truth but tell it slant."

"Splitting Wood", p. 67
Somewhere I read that to bring the right amount of force down on the log you're splitting, you ought to aim at the block, not the log. That seems to me to be a technique rich with wisdom for poetry and life.

"Spring in Late Summer", p. 69
What I'd thought a new spring: alludes to an incident reported in my poem "A Spring & A Heron," in *Walking Underwater*.
Undine has dwindled into her undone poet's remains: the poet Seamus Heaney had died not long before, and these two poems remember him. Undine (or Ondine) is a water nymph, birthed in Greek mythology and spoken of by Ovid in *Metamorphoses*. Her doom is to fall in love with

a mortal, but will die if he is unfaithful. Ravel and Debussy both wrote music with this myth in mind. Seamus Heaney wrote a poem "Undine," from the point of view of the nymph herself.

"Night Lies", p. 72
This poem has taken several different shapes over many years. I settled on a short haibun: haiku–prose-poem–haiku.
I fall asleep with Amy Lowell and wake with Jay Parini: I was reading some Amy Lowell poems at the time, along with Jay Parini's *Why Poetry Matters*, Yale, 2009.

"She & I", p. 73
On his walk / to the gallows, the condemned man steps around a puddle: George Orwell's essay "A Hanging" includes this detail and a reflection on it.
The solid form / Of that great Babylon of languages: Robert Bringhurst, *The Solid Form of Language*, Gaspereau, 2016.

"No Words", p. 75
The quoted words with which this poem begins came, I believe, from a song or poem. In my distraction at and after that time, I mislaid the quote and haven't been able to find it. (I may have woken with the phrase in my head.) One possible source is the song by Dotan, "No Words"; another some words on grief attributed to Dawn Dais: "When there are no words, know that the silences are carrying the thoughts and prayers of all who love you," words I may have read on a card sent to me, or words I may have happened on in her book *The Sh!t No One Tells You*, at the house of my friends, Ed and Holly. Thank you whoever it was whose words gave me the poem, which gave me some solace.

"Welcome Swallows", p. 78
A sonnet I wrote at Bundanon in 2010.
Making nothing happen: W H Auden's well known and widely misinterpreted words from his poem "In Memory of W B Yeats": "For poetry makes nothing happen."

"Colour Theory", p. 80
Although it makes reference to many people, mostly poets (and my child), and to criticism in

The New Yorker, I think this free-verse poem more or less speaks for itself.

"The Child & Time", p. 83
For some years, this poem, written mostly about and for my son Henry, hung in the hall of the family home. It was the poem, before that, that won my first prize, the Gwen Harwood (2005), and it convinced me I might be a poet. It may have been my first published poem, too: it appeared in *Island* in September 2006. I have held off putting it in a collection until now. Its ideas fit my themes here—beginnings, art-making, life-making, time. Think about this, given its interest in what changes and what stays: the boy in the poem has just entered university.

"You Know How This Goes", p. 88
Vincent had it right: Vincent Van Gogh, of course. The italicised words are from his letters.
The thing with feathers: Emily Dickinson.

"The End of Poetry (As We Know It to Be)", p. 91
My one and, so far, only, piece of rap. Mercifully short.

"Amen: A Moment of the World", p. 92
I wrote this poem in response to a commission from Miriam Hechtman to respond to the letter A in relation to masculinity, for a book she's editing: *An Alphabet of Men*, a follow up to her *An Alphabet of Women*, from late 2021.

"The World is Here for its Own Delight", p. 97
I take the title of this sonnet from an anthology of spiritual poetry, edited by Robert Bly: *The Soul Is Here for Its Own Joy*. Bly's title is itself drawn from a poem by Rumi, translated by Coleman Barks.

"Ubirr", p. 98
Still my only villanelle, this poem was shortlisted for a prize before I knew I could write poetry. Ubirr is a rock outcrop of deep spiritual significance to the Bininj and Mungguy, whose lands these are: a gallery of Indigenous rock art, in Kakadu National Park, in the far north of the Northern Territory. It looks across the Nadab floodplain. The day I visited was the last day

buses ran there, ahead of the anticipated wet season. And standing on the rock, I watched the Wet roll in, as the poem describes. We drove back to Darwin in a downpour. The poem begins with an epigraph, from a poem by Bill Neidjie, whose lands, I believe these are.

"Gaudeamus Igitur", p. 100
The Latin phrase of my title, which translates as "So, Let Us Rejoice," seems to have come into use in the late 1200s in Europe—an exhortation to get on with life. It is best known as part of the Academic anthem, "*De Brevitate Vitae*." My poem—a gift of thanks to Barry Lopez, for having us stay at his place in the Cascades, near Eugene, Oregon, in early 2020—takes the form of a pair of sijo. Barry had told a story of hearing a Russian choir sing the Gaudeamus in a solemn, but gorgeous arrangement, at a literary festival in, I think, Australia, and he spoke of that as the spirit in which we must face up to the coming climate catastrophe. By September that year, Barry had lost the guesthouse/studio we slept in and many of his papers and artworks and books in a fire, the first he had ever known along the cool, damp river valley I describe in the poem. That event seemed to break him, and by Christmas, he was dead. This poem rejoices in his life and work.

"Lichen", p. 103
The sculpture I stumbled on is "Reclining Figure," by Olavi Lanu, on the campus of the Australian National University.

"Two Tanka for BL", p. 104
Two small poems I wrote in December 2021 as Barry Lopez spent his last days in a hospice in Oregon. Digitally, at least, Barry was able to hear what his friends thought of him, including these two tanka.

"Outside", p. 105
An elegy for Barry Lopez, after his passing, employing a nine-by-nine by nine.
"Outside" is the title of a selection of Barry Lopez's stories. I took it out and read it again, outside, in the months after his death. I found several feathers interleaved in it, and I seem to recall Barry had put them there. Walking on those days, I kept finding feathers fallen wherever I went. I carried many home and pressed them in the book. In one of the stories, "Within Birds' Hear-

ing," I read "Hope has become a bird's feather, glissading from the evening sky." This will explain some of the references in the poem.
Cantus in memoriam: because one of Barry Lopez's favourite pieces of music was Arvo Part's "Cantus in memoriam Benjamin Britten." It made, he told me once, the sound he wished his writing could make.

"We Are Not Finished at the Skin", p. 109
The title is a phrase of Barry Lopez's, words I quoted from him in the chapter "The Edge of the Trees," in *The Land's Wild Music*, 2004, Trinity University Press. With the photographer, Lucia Rossi, I presented a spoken version of this poem, at a conference in Hobart in early 2007.

"Five Soft Nets", p. 119
This sooty-oyster-captured place, along / This whalebone shore: sooty oystercatchers frequent the rockshelf at Coledale and along the south coast of New South Wales. A Wodi Wodi story identifies Coledale with whales and whale strandings.
Rags of time: John Donne, "The Sunne Rising".
Merrigong: the Wodi Wodi name for the eastern escarpment that runs close to the coast at Coledale.
And spelling mistakes: Coledale is widely understood to be a misspelling of Coal Dale.
Forty-seven colourful false starts: I have in mind Janet Malcolm's essay, "Forty-One False Starts."
My mother, it happens, was born in these measures: at Helensburgh.
Coal spells many things / And only some of them well: another allusion to the misspelling in the name, but also a suggestion of all that has not gone well because of coal.
Round-cornered world: John Donne's sonnet "At the round earths imagin'd corners".
The whole contracted / Thus: Donne again: "In that the world's contracted thus," in "The Sunne Rising."
A place is a mind / You may come to share: from my essay "Nourishing Terrains", *Sydney Review of Books*, September 2018.

"South Coast Sedoka", p. 127
This and a number of the poems through this section bear witness to Dolphin Point and Sanctuary Point and places on the mid-South Coast of New South Wales. Sedoka is a Japanese form,

a variant on the haiku: three-line poems, of radical compression, employing lines of some combination of 5, 7, and 7 syllables. They are supposed to contain or answer a question, shared with the beloved.

"Among the Lighted Woods with Dante", p. 128
The title invokes Dante Alighieri, of course, and indeed, there was a little finding of one's self in woods, but I was with my love, and the name of our pup is Dante, so I am fooling with you. Except that Jodie and I were reading Dante during this time in the house by Erowal, while we all reckoned with the first year of the pandemic. So there is a real sense of the *selva oscura* about the poem.

"Ghazal of the Weather Upon the Lake", p. 130
I wrote this poem in response to a commission from Peter Lustig, to whom it's commissioned. I chose the ghazal form because it seemed apt for the idea of the contrapuntal nature of things that I wanted to get at. I teach the ghazal, and I honour it as an old form, used continuously in the parts of the world we like, in the West, to call the Middle East. The song of the cornered ghazal expresses abject love, abandonment, regret for better, truer times passed. The contradiction of things. Mine attempts some of the traditional constraints of the form: sustained couplets of identical syllabic length; a rhyme scheme; a (very oblique) naming of the poet in the final line. Thank you, Peter, for the gig. And I hope I have paid homage to the form.

"Flat Rock, September", p. 133
This poem employs a shape I admired in a poem written for my masterclass by Rona Shaeffer, although my voicing and setting and ideation are altogether other than hers. The poem, which shortlisted for the 2021 Blake Poetry Prize, bears witness to an epiphanic moment on the Upper Kangaroo River one recent September, where my daughter had insisted we go and swim. The waterhole is sacred—you can tell that just by being there. It turns out it is a women's site, sacred to the mothers and daughters of the Indigenous people (the Wodi Wodi) whose place this is. Perhaps life and love and time run more like chains of ponds than rivers, each pond an ephemeral pool that never empties out. This was such a moment, of healing between me and my children and of birth, rebirth and dying at the end of day. It speaks sorrow for dispossession enacted here; it hopes for "honour among us thieves"; it says thanks "for lives that

float a while yet." I want to thank friend and poetry mentee Brigitte Ross, a long time Kangaroo Valley local, for first mentioning the site to me.

"The Hill Again", p. 139
This is set on Hammock Hill, near where I used often to walk, sometimes with the dog (see "On Hammock Hill," in *Bluewren Cantos*), near Bowral. On a return visit after the end of a marriage.

"Up", p. 143
A poem from Newcastle on the Hunter, Awakabal and Worimi lands, where I lived, four flights up, and above the port for a year or so.

"Wait" and **"The Hill"**, p. 145-6
Poems written on or near "The Hill," where I lived that year in an apartment like a treehouse.

"The Halflife of Coal", p. 147
This poem, which engages, in three parts, with three sites of archaeological interest in and around the city of Newcastle, was commissioned by The Lockup in Newcastle and included in "Brought to Light," a multi-arts installation, 2010. "Above" deals in and transacts some details about the dilapidated house of the Supervisor of Mines; "Between," with the Empire Baths, ocean baths, which you can still make out in remnants on the rock shelf at Newcastle Main Beach; "Below", the Soldiers' Baths which can now be found by descending stairs from Hunter Street.
There is no blue without yellow: a letter Vincent Van Gogh wrote to his brother Theo.
Charles Milligan Little: last inhabitant of the house.
Many references in "Below" sample and riff names and places from the *Egyptian Book of the Dead* and make other allusions to Dante's *Comedia*.

"Revelation Days", p. 152
A response to the fires that burned great swathes of the southeast coastal forests of Australia in the summer of 2019–20, this poem was also a gift of thanks to poet Alison Whitelock and her partner Thomas, who had had us stay with them a couple of days, days when a little rain finally

fell, on the coast south of Sydney.
Darling showers: dust storms.

"Above the Snowies on the Day of First Snow", p. 154
The Snowy Mountains, and other ranges of the Great Divide, on a flight from Sydney to Melbourne.

"The Jetty", p. 155
A poem written for the Busselton Jetty in southwestern Western Australia, part of a project, managed by Donna Ward, editor of *Indigo Journal*, to commemorate the old wharf and mark the new one.

"The Bay", p. 158
As should be clear, the poem is written in Fiji, where I ran a writing workshop once.

"Jimbaran Bay, Late October", p. 160
Along the shore the women/ Come and go, speaking of Pialago: Riffs on T S Eliot's "Love Song of J Alfred Prufrock": "In the room, the women come and go/ Talking of Michelangelo."
Pialago: a suburb of Canberra, close to the airport. A Ngunnawal word, said to mean "I'll tell you in a while."
I was in Bali for the Ubud Writers Festival.

"At My Brother's House", p. 161
Another Bali poem, for my friend and host, John Sullivan.

"Tropicbird", p. 162
This poem, set on Bali, reports and merges two dreams.

"Late Spring Snow, Reno", p. 163
One of a number of poems I wrote on an extended tour of the US and Canada in 2011, when I was the poet in residence at the University of Nebraska, as a guest of the Great Plains Institute. This one is written in the library of the University of Nevada, Reno, where, as a guest of Pro-

fessor Scott Slovic, pioneer of ecocriticism, I had made a guest lecture.

"Basin & Range", p. 165
I draw my title—for a poem written after some time in Nevada, flying across that state, its basins and ranges, toward New York—from John McPhee's Basin and Range, one of his five books on the geology of the continent on which the USA sits. William Fox, director, Center for Art + Environment at the university, and the author of many books in geography and culture of the southwest, had driven me out into the Nevada deserts the weekend before I flew.

"Grace", p. 166
I wrote the first draft of this poem sitting in the Sheldon Museum of Art on the campus of the University of Nebraska, Lincoln, killing time before a guest lecture. There was an exhibition of still life paintings ("Poetical Fire") in the Rain Gallery near where I sat, and as I sat, a choir came in and sang, a rehearsal, in the vaulted space, and the poem records how that went and how it felt. I got so caught in the music and the poem, I had to run to my lecture in the English Department, and when I entered, I found an expectant crowd, to whom I read the poem I'd just written. I'm not sure what Ted Kooser, Poet Laureate and emeritus professor at the university, made of it, for he was sitting in the front row and made no comment to me after.

"Fifty Words (or more) for Snow", p. 167
In early 2020, I ran a poetry masterclass, "Fire & Ice," in Quebec, organised by the poet Lise Rochefort. This poem was written there and is a gift for her and Adrian.

"Puck", p. 168
Written about the beginning of a four-day train trip from Vancouver to Montreal, after the flight from Sydney, which arrived earlier than I left. Watching ice hockey in a state of profound sleep-deficit made it even more obscure than it otherwise might have been. I had spent the afternoon at the art gallery, which explains some of the references in "slow puck", and the reflections I fall into on the theme of love.

"The Wild Life of Southern Ontario", p. 170
Another Canadian train poem.

"Ontario Slides", p. 172
Canadian Train Poem #3. Seems I'm heading from Toronto to Ottawa here.

"Inside Passage, Sunday Morning", p. 174
On the ferry from Victoria to Vancouver. March or April 2011.

"Halfway Home", p. 175
A poem that witnesses an extended-play reverie, such as one has on longhaul flights; mine was a flight from Vancouver to Sydney, April 2012.
Aeneas on a string: I'm thinking, as the next line betrays (*mythic and elegant as Virgilian hexameter*), about Virgil's *Aeneid*, and the long homeward journey, through various tests of heart and body, of its protagonist.

"Rain at Eltham", p. 177
Eltham is a pastoral suburb in the hills northeast of Melbourne, in the shire of Nillumbik. There is a fabulous bookstore there, which runs, or once did, its own literary festival, at which I was a guest once or twice. I spent a week in 2009, I think, in accommodation run by Gwen Ford in a garden designed by her husband Gordon Ford. I wrote a book and I wrote a few poems, and this was one. It shortlisted for the Rosemary Dobson poetry prize.

"Along the River Tonight", p. 179
The poem is set in Picton, New South Wales, where I lived on a couple of occasions. The creek beside the track is the Stonequarry Creek.

"Doing the Numbers: 02/01/2017", p. 183
This one, a birthday meditation, is set in the Dandenongs, near Belgrave.

"January Poplars", p. 185
A late January meditation remembering a house I once lived in, a shed I once wrote in, and the water poplars I once looked out on. I was reading that summer all the entries, the 142 books, in the nonfiction category of the NSW Premier's Literary Prize.

"Mecca", p. 187
Not long before I found myself sitting in a "Mecca," a cafe on King Street, Sydney, ahead of a two-day business-writing course, taught in the Grace Hotel, the premier of the state had said words like those I attribute to him here. A nice moment in political discourse, before it dwindled even deeper into the soulless cant it has become.

"Balmain Nocturne", p. 189
Balmain, Sydney. This nocturne is also a kind of anticipatory aubade.

"With Sarasvati Under the Lemon-Scented Gum Tonight", p. 190
Another Balmain nocturne.

"Blues Point Blues", p. 191
A Lavender Bay aubade. Lavender Bay, where I have lived a couple of times, was frequently painted by Brett Whitely. Picture one of his canvases for the background setting here.

"The Cycles of the Moon", p. 192
This accidental series on the moon pictures the same moon in different stages, on the Bong Bong Flats, in Balmain, in Melbourne, at Queenscliff, in Cremorne. It gets around, that moon, "chaste wastrel."

"Yours Tonight", p. 198
The moon again: and a child (Henry, I think), and a nocturne in the form of a prose poem, on the theme of nostalgia and endings.
Sharon Olds: I quote from her poem "Unspeakable."

"A Death in the Family", p. 199
The poem's references explain themselves in the poem. The poet drives home from Sydney to Bowral, where home lay.
Samuel Barber's lullaby: "Knoxville: Summer 1915": a work for voice and orchestra, by Samuel Barber, 1947. Commissioned by soprano Eleanor Steber and first sung in 1948.

James Agee's uncanny prose: the prose poem was first published in 1938 when Agee was 28. It recalls a night when he was five. Agee included it as the prologue to his novel *A Death in the Family*, begun in 1948 and not quite finished in 1955, when he died. The novel, edited and finished by David McDowell, came out in 1957.

"Flash Fiction", p. 200
Sometimes fiction bears a close relationship to fact; sometimes not. And as Robert Gray once told me: "if poetry isn't fiction, it should be."

"Three Shadows", p. 201
A Picton prose poem.

"Body Copy", p. 205
For a long time, this was the working title of this book.
The publisher, typographer in me likes the play between "title" and "body copy." The book moved a little away from the mood of this poem, but here are the central concerns of beginning, and beginning again and of being in the body of the world. The poem is set at the Cecil Hoskins Reserve, where a number of my poems wander.

"In Medias Res", p. 207
Poet's dark wood…straight way was lost: I have in mind the start of Dante's *Comedia*.
The woods weren't lovely: I have in mind Frost's "Stopping by Woods on a Winter Evening".
In medias res: "Into the middle of things"; used, first by Roman poet Horace in his *ars poetica* (13 BC) to describe a literary technique of beginning narrative without preamble, in the middle of the action. Hence my *Horace's Latin*.
Panther in a zoo: Rilke's "Der Panther" (1902).

"Catullus, at Dusk, Lustful and Heartbroken, Tries His Hand at Haiku", p. 209
A haiku whose title (and haiku oughtn't to have titles) is, itself, a haiku.
Catullus: Roman poet (84–54BC), famous for poems of almost abject devotion to a lover who was indifferent to him; remembered, too, for the frank sexuality of his poems and their fierce political criticism.

Household gods: in Classical Rome the *lares* and *penates*, household deities, often occupied the mantel, from where they oversaw the fortunes of the house.

"Youth: A Second Coming", p. 212
The tenderness. The slenderness: Matsuo Basho wrote that a good poem should be "tender, slender, and lonely."
My poem also has in mind Derek Walcott's "Love After Love."

"Fish Me Up Plural", p. 214
"There is a way of passing away from the personal, a dying that makes one plural": Rumi (trans. Coleman Barks). This idea runs through my poem.

"At Night the House", p. 219
Set, like all the sestets in this part, in Bowral. "Your Voice" is the exception: it imagines a beach in Jervis Bay and remembers an old love.

"Bach, or is it Ravel?", p. 220
I lived at that time with my grandmother's piano. In my childhood, my grandmother, Rachel Marks, lived with us, in a flat attached to our family home, and this piano lived with her, and we lived, mostly happily, with the sound of her playing it. The entirety of her repertoire was the Methodist hymn book. The incident described in the poem happened.

"Landscape with Laptop", p. 229
Like old words fallen overnight out of use: "They were like certain old words that today are going out of use": John Berger, "A Bunch of Flowers in a Glass", *Photocopies*, 1996.
Into that first place you left so long ago: "apokatastasis", or, the way things seem in our minds to have stood originally; a state of original wholeness. See Tim Lilburn's discussion of this in his *Living in the World as if it were Home*, which I was reading at the time I wrote this poem. The poem runs from Chinaman's to Hyam's Beach and back.

"Among Trees", p. 234
This poem is set in the Margaret River region of southwestern Australia.

Full beyond words: this phrase and the weather of the last line and a half come from James Salter's *Light Years*.

"Fog Lies", p. 236
Reports a drive to Canberra in thick fog, one early morning.
Parched and apostate lake: Weereewa (Lake George).

"One AM Sublime", p. 238
A Bowral nocturne, from when the children were young.

"At Home on a Sunday Trying to Find Nothing to Do", p. 242
Temple of the word: the Chinese pictograph for "poetry" translates roughly as "the temple of the word".
Let the morning come: the poem invokes and responds to Jane Kenyon's "Let Evening Come."

"April into May", p. 245
A poem written in the cowshed at Bowral, thinking about love and reading and place.
Some very smart worlds on fire: "the world/ is a word on fire that you have to hold": William Stafford, "What to Say."

"Transit of Venus", p. 252
A poem, written in the cowshed, reporting the astrological and terrestrial weather of some fairly "numinous days."

"What Happens if the Heart is Not Where the Home Is?", p. 253
Another Bowral poem, contemplating the art of belonging where you don't love being.

"Break & Enter", p. 255
A poem written in the shed and contemplating the beautiful strangeness of a rose growing outside, but flowering inside the glass. Maree my then wife, loved and cultivated roses, including the one in the poem.
Camille Pisarro: the name of the rose in question; also the name of a pointillist painter of the

nineteenth century, for whom the rose is named.
Something there is… that does not love… : I'm riffing on Robert Frost's line: "Something there is that does not love a wall," from "Mending Wall."

"Old Beginnings", p. 257
The poem is set in the cowshed again, after beginning at the Cecil Hoskins Reserve.

"Winter Comes in Overnight", p. 268
A poem I began in Picton and finished in Bowral.

"The Moon is Round and Fires Ring", p. 269
A poem written is September or October, after years of drought, just ahead of the fires of 2019.

"Cicada Sonnet", p. 270
Rowers in Eden: "rowing in Eden," from "Wild Nights—Wild Nights!" (269) by Emily Dickinson.

"Black Swan Moment", p. 271
The phrase "black swan moment" came into vogue for a while there. I guess it arose in the Northern Hemisphere, where not only is it true that all swans are white, but also the proposition that "all swans are white" was taught, in England anyway, as an instance of a self-evident presumption in philosophy. But in Australia all swans, until others were introduced, were always black. That discovery, for Banks or whoever it was, was the original black swan moment. All of that lies behind this poem, a love sonnet on the theme of refusal to conform, which also observes the flash of white inside the black swan's wings, which is, I guess, a white wing moment.

"Comes a Time", p. 272
A poem begun in Canberra, continued on the road home, past Weereewa (Lake George), empty at that time, and finished in rising hope on Station Street, Picton, home then.
The moment is an empty lake: Weereewa.
Argyle apples: a favourite tree, the one species (or one of two or three) that keeps its blue-grey leaves all its life. One grew near my home in Picton.

"Nine Pines on Kangaloon", p. 277

The poem is an elegy for Deborah Bird Rose. It was commissioned by Stuart Cooke and Peter Boyle for an anthology they pulled together for Deb, as she faced her last months. She is the friend I allude to in the poem.

Kangaloon: the name of the road my house at that time fronted. There were nine pines along the frontage of that house. Kangaloon is also the name of a wetland, dammed to make a reservoir—the water the Southern Highlands drinks. Deb and Freya Mathews and I visited that swamp and performed a small ritual there, because we took its name for a group of us, poets and humanities scholars, concerned to make a contribution, though art, to the conversation about climate change.

The poem includes many references to Deb's life and thought and work, to that fellowship of scholars, whose animating spirit Deb was, and to that house on Kangaloon, its liquidambar, its pines.

"All the Campbelltowns", p. 281

I wrote this poem to use at an event I was speaking at for WestWords. I believe it was the opening of the Wedderburn office—Wedderburn is near Campbelltown, New South Wales. Later I ran that office for WestWords for a while, and, among other things, a number of poems arose in that setting. Wedderburn and Campbelltown are Dharawal country, and I make a number of references to plants and trees and fish that characterise that country—Macquarie Perch, petrophile, bluewren, geebungs.

Blaxland Road, where I had been walking not long before, runs near Campbelltown, at Lumeah.

Wollondilly: the river that defines the district (and the name of the shire).

Picton hills: or the Razorback; near where I then lived; prominent in the topography and culture of the region.

The poem is for my son Daniel, because I wrote the end of it while I watched him play basketball that morning; and it's for Michelle Rickerby, who was my colleague at WestWords, and the reason I worked there a while.

"The Schoolhouse", p. 283

The office of WestWords, in Wedderburn, where I worked for a time, was a schoolhouse, first put up in the late nineteen-hundreds. This poem describes a day there and reflects on some of the social and natural history of the school.

"The Teacher", p. 284
I wrote this poem on commission for the high school I went to, on the occasion of the retirement of its headmaster, who had been my English teacher.
The readiness was always all: "The readiness is all": William Shakespeare, Hamlet, Act 5; scene 2.
The play was always the thing: "the play's the thing": William Shakespeare, Hamlet, Act 2; scene 2.
A schoolboy, a lover, a (tin) soldier: Roderick Kefford, "The Schoolboy, the Lover, and the Soldier: A Study of the Problems Reported by Economically-privileged Australian-born Adolescent Males," *The Australian Teacher*, 1972.
Each of us, the other, if you reach down far enough: I echo Charles Wright's "everyone's life is the same life, if you live long enough," from "The Southern Cross."

"Spring", p. 287
Alan Holley, friend and composer, commissioned this poem from me as a gift he and some friends would give their friend John Edmonds, lover of poetry and music.
My glory, said a poet once: W B Yeats, "The Municipal Gallery Revisited."

"The Iris", p. 289
Along the creek, the cherry trees: the Cherry Tree Walk, close to my parents' home.
Trumpets in the flue pipes, pigeons at the pedals... : my mother is an organist. Hence the musical and organ references here.
Phosphorescence: my mother loved Julia Baird's book of that name, a title drawn in turn from Emily Dickinson.
A happy cipher: a cipher is a ghostly, inadvertent sound in the pipes of an organ.

"Holding My Father's Heart", p. 291
A poem for my father on his ninetieth birthday. The poem is written in terza rima, although it insisted on a tetrametric beat. Joshua Yeldham's painting was my inspiration.

"The Gardens of Beijing", p. 304
I wrote this sequence in April 2019, when I was a guest of the Lu Xun Academy's International Writers Program.
"Peace Piece": Bill Evans' composition and performance.

"I am My Beloved's, & My Beloved is Mine", p. 313
This was for my brother Rohan and his bride Mariza on their wedding day. The poem, including its title, samples phrases and images from "The Song of Songs": *the rose of Sharon; the apple among the trees of the wood; the winter is past, the rain is over and gone; the time of the singing of birds; Come, my beloved, let us go forth into the field* (from "Rise up, my love, my fair one, and come away"); and *love is strong as death.*

"Imagine an Afternoon", p. 315
My title draws on the opening sentence of a story by Truman Capote, "A Christmas Memory": "Imagine a morning in late November."

"Why You're Here", p. 316
I wrote this with my daughter Louisa in mind (though she scarcely needed it). But it is a speaking to that lost child in my self and all our selves. It offers an answer to the deep questions we carry in, and about our lives: why do I live, how should I live, what is my life?

"Page One", p. 323
A poem that celebrates my partner, Jodie Williams, and her returning to the piano at fifty, nearly forty years after she last played it.
Page one of each a corner you're not ready yet to turn: a joke we shared about the way Jodie would master each new piece she turned to, but only as far as page one.
Each a piece of an antique peace: a reference to Bill Evans's "Peace Piece," which Jodie learned to play after we heard it (again, in my case) in a café in Shilipu, Beijing.

Painting by Michael Henderson

MARK TREDINNICK: *A brief life*

Dr MARK TREDINNICK BA (Hons), LLB (Hons), MBA, PhD—is a celebrated poet, essayist, and teacher. His many works of poetry and prose include *A Gathered Distance*, *Almost Everything I Know*, *Egret in a Ploughed Field*, *Bluewren Cantos*, *Fire Diary*, *The Blue Plateau*, and *The Little Red Writing Book*. For twenty-five years, he's taught poetry and expressive writing at the University of Sydney, where he was poet in residence in 2018. His many honours include two Premier's Book Awards, and two of the world's foremost poetry prizes, the Montreal and the Cardiff. "His is a bold, big-thinking poetry," Sir Andrew Motion has written, "in which ancient themes (especially the theme of our human relationship with landscape) are recast and rekindled." "One of our great poets of place," Judy Beveridge has called him.

In 2020, Mark Tredinnick was awarded the Order of Australia Medal for services to literature and education.

His last book, *Walking Underwater*, was published by Pitt Street Poetry in September 2021; *A Beginner's Guide* is Tredinnick's fifth collection, and it appears in his sixty-first year. He's at work on a book of prose and poetry about the Great Divide, the lyrics for a passion, and a collection of essays.

Tredinnick's work has been widely translated—into Chinese, Spanish, French, Italian, and German. In 2019, he spent a month in Beijing as a guest of the China Writers international writers' program. In 2021, Mark won the first ever Miluo River International Poetry Prize, for his poem "Before the Day." A collection of his poems and essays appears in translation in China in 2023.

Mark is the father of five, and he lives with his partner Jodie Williams, their spaniels Dante and Carlos and their cat Sappho, in Gundungurra country, along the Wingecarribee, southwest of Sydney. In 2020 Mark launched his online poetry masterclass series, *What the Light Tells*. For more: marktredinnick.com.

Books

Poetry

Walking Underwater, Pitt Street Poetry, 2021
A Gathered Distance, Birdfish Books, 2020
So Far, Birdfish Books, 2019
Egret in a Ploughed Field, Chinese University Press, 2017
Anthology: Gardening the Future: An Essay in Plants, Poetry and Image, TCL, 2017
The Lyrebird & Other Poems (2e), Ginninderra, 2017
Almost Everything I Know, Flying Island, 2015
Bluewren Cantos, Pitt Street Poetry, 2013
Fire Diary (2e), Pitt Street Poetry, 2014
Australian Love Poems 2013 (Ed), Inkerman & Blunt, 2013
The Lyrebird (Wagtail 106), Picaro, 2011
Fire Diary, Puncher & Wattmann, 2010
The Road South (CD), River Road, 2008

Prose

Australia's Wild Weather, NLA, 2011
The Blue Plateau, UQP/Milkweed, 2009
The Land's Wild Music, Trinity, 2005
A Place on Earth (Ed), UNSW/U Nebraska, 2003/04

Books on Writing

The Little Black Book of Business Writing, New South, 2009 (With Geoff Whyte)
The Little Green Grammar Book, New South, 2008
The Little Red Writing Book, New South, 2006

Praise for Mark Tredinnick

"Mark Tredinnick's are among the only long poems I find myself actively wanting to read. A few others these days can write well at length, but not many. Mark's cadences bring the sense of a vertebrae meter, or perhaps of a keel, giving each poem the feel of a well-balanced canoe, sound enough to navigate deftly larger waters."

—Jane Hirshfield

"His is a bold, big-thinking poetry, in which ancient themes (especially the theme of our human relationship with landscape) are recast and rekindled."

—Andrew Motion

"He has a tenderly erotic way of taking things. Every poem is a love poem."

—Philip Gross

"Mark Tredinnick is one of our great poets of place—not just of geographic place, but of the spiritual and moral landscapes as well. His are poems of vision and affirming wisdom."

—Judith Beveridge

Praise for *A Beginner's Guide*

"Mark Tredinnick's poems find the beauty in the hard places."

—Debbie Lim

"*A Beginner's Guide* conditions us to calibrate our listening beyond our daily lives to 'the silence that's been running / Under all our selves.' There, he reveals, in each poem and line and song, is a hewn strength of human feeling that transports us to 'a grove and groove' of wonder and light."

—Major Jackson

"Both precise and expansive, Mark Tredinnick's poetry demonstrates not only exceptional control of a difficult craft, but also a singular awareness of its moral weight. Each poem in this collection, like each moment we have in life, feels like the chance of a new beginning."

—John Foulcher

"Sublime, tender & almost holy, these poems allow us '*at last, to stand in the light of the world*'.

—Ali Whitelock

"These poems weaponise grace. On every page of *A Beginner's Guide*, Mark Tredinnick renders rivers, birds and dogs, the sheoaks, frogs and all the swarming insects and stars with a vividness most poets reserve for human love affairs. A deep connection with Country is the wild root of all these poems—so rare in non-Indigenous poets, and so important."

—Judith Nangala Crispin

"Mark Tredinnick's tender love poems to life and land are a tonic for tough times. *A Beginner's Guide* is a generous collection from a confident, freewheeling navigator of the inner and the outer worlds."

—Lisa Brockwell

"This intimate collection of poems is a profound journey of the senses. Exquisite ceremonies of observation, meditation, and wonder."

—Didi Jackson

www.ingramcontent.com/pod-product-compliance
Lightning Source LLC
Chambersburg PA
CBHW060522010526
44107CB00060B/2660